D1114824

JACOB'S NIGHT

Jacob's Struggle with the Angel

JACOB'S NIGHT

The Religious Renascence
in France

BY
WALLACE FOWLIE

NEW YORK

SHEED & WARD

1947

TO

CATHERINE COFFIN

ACKNOWLEDGMENTS

WE WISH to acknowledge the courtesy of Mr. T. S. Eliot and of Harcourt, Brace and Company, Inc., in permitting us to use the excerpts from *The Wasteland, Anabase,* and *Four Quartets* quoted in this book.

CONTENTS

I   PÉGUY: *The Presence of a Prophet*   1

II   ROUAULT: *The Art of a Painter*   25

III   MARITAIN: *The Message of a Philosopher*   53

IV   *Myths of Modern Poetry*   77

       NOTES   103

       THE FRONTISPIECE: Gauguin, *Jacob and the Angel*   105

       NOTE I: *Existentialist Theatre*   106

       NOTE II: *The Example of Max Jacob*   111

    INDEX   115

I · Péguy

THE PRESENCE OF A PROPHET

PÉGUY:

The Presence of a Prophet

ANY CONSIDERATION of the religious renascence in contemporary France leads one back inevitably to the example and the work of Charles Péguy. The "presence of Péguy" is a subject which almost imposes itself today as a kind of affectionate duty toward France. During the war years and since the war, friends of France who are in every country of the world, and especially perhaps in England and America, have thought ceaselessly of the seeming insurmountable difficulties of food distribution, as well as of the problems of morale and politics. More perhaps than of these, they have been thinking of the destiny of France. Péguy, better than all other modern writers, can help us to approach France, to feel her problems and to see, beyond the spiritual myopia of modern times, the gradually re-forming elements of her destiny.

This fact of the continued presence of Péguy is almost miraculous, because he died in September 1914, at the beginning of the other war. During the period between the two wars, Péguy was read by a small, limited public

3

but one which was fervently devoted to him. Then during the German occupation years, the number of his readers continued to increase to a marked degree. Today in France, Péguy is almost venerated. He has become, if not a saint, at least a very sacred symbol of France. Each period chooses its saints and representatives. Péguy's work, which is vast and difficult in many ways to read, stands out already as the most essential testimonial of an entire period.

During the five recent years of war, the radio and the newspapers kept us informed of all the material trials which France was undergoing. We were told about malnutrition, lack of medicine, the shells which rained on certain cities, the children who were dying of tuberculosis. But all that was nothing by comparison with the moral suffering of the French, with the feeling of shame which oppressed them, with the enemy's effort to change the French, even in their manner of thinking, in their conscience and their morality. I imagine that it was in this moral struggle, the most difficult of all, that Péguy was able to intervene. We cannot yet judge the rôle of Péguy in French thought, but we are convinced that his work will occupy one of the first places in the history of literature. Catastrophes were necessary—and sufficiently cosmic in order to shatter all the forms of modern optimism—for Péguy's work to be revealed and justified.

Buried in the heart of one of his longest works is a very small sentence, or rather a prayer, which serves as a key to the thought of this man. The title of the work:

Le Porche du mystère de la deuxième vertu, is very long. In fact much longer than the brief prayer which I am going to quote because it explains the entire work and life of Péguy. And I repeat it now because it has filled the hearts of the French during these recent difficult years: *"Il faut que France continue."* ("France must continue.") This is the central sentence of Péguy's long work on hope. The work deals with the second of the great theological virtues: hope, which comes after faith and before charity. No one has spoken so eloquently as Péguy has on the theme of hope, which is for him the eminently French virtue, *"la petite espérance,"* as he called it, and which usually appeared to him in the guise of a little girl.

(1)

It is not my intention to relate the life story of Charles Péguy. This story has become almost legendary, and has been told in such detail in books and lectures that if I attempted to summarize it here, I should probably not reach the aspect of his work which I want especially to consider. And yet, I cannot begin my subject without devoting a short space to a discussion of the beginnings of his life. Péguy has written extensively about his life, his origins, his native city. In all that he has written about himself, one brief sentence has always particularly struck me. It is in his book *L'Argent: "Tout est joué avant que nous ayons douze ans."* ("Everything is cast before we are twelve.")

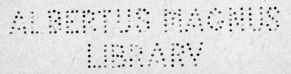

The very earliest years—and I believe that psychologists tell us today the very first weeks—profoundly influence and determine a human being. Péguy was born in the old city of Orléans, where he was raised by two women, his mother and his grandmother, two women of the people who all their lives struggled on the frontier of poverty. His mother repaired the straw seats of chairs, and Péguy always thought of himself as being the son of the chair-maker (*le gars de la rempailleuse*). He was proud of his mother's work, which he called the intermediary trade between heavy and refined work. The mother long survived her son, since she died in January 1933, at the age of eighty-six. Until her death (and all the time receiving visitors from Paris who were curious to see this woman of whom Péguy had written so often in his books) she continued, through habit and fidelity, to weave the straw seats of chairs.

From her Péguy inherited especially his natural dignity, his peasant pride. It is not difficult to imagine the grave countenance of the child, of the small boy dressed, as are all the sons of the people, in his black apron, in heavy, iron-clad shoes and a cap with gold braid. I do not believe that Péguy ever felt deep love for his mother, who did not have a very flexible temperament. He felt respect and admiration for her. But his first love, and his last also, was for his studies and his primary school classes. Péguy's greatest passion was that of knowing and understanding. This very pure passion in childhood marked and safeguarded Péguy's moral purity throughout his life.

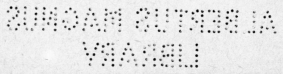

As a child Péguy followed two kinds of study: the first, directed by the lay masters, in what he often called "that admirable world of primary school education" (*"cet admirable monde de l'enseignement primaire"*) and the second, directed by the Catholic masters, the catechism classes. Two kinds of education, the first distributed by the Republic and the second by the Church. And even as a child Péguy recognized that these two educations were diametrically opposed. But he learned his catechism as impeccably as the lessons of primary school.

"We were," he used to say, "small serious boys in that serious city." (*"Nous étions des petits garçons sérieux de cette ville sérieuse."*) This first portrait which Péguy gives us of himself as that of a small, serious youngster is authentic. "People never change" (*"on ne change jamais"*), he says in the same passage. And that is why I have begun with these few words on the first years of Charles Péguy in the city of Orléans, where he took everything seriously, both what his lay masters taught him and what his priests taught him. There he learned especially how to take work seriously. "To work is to pray," he used to write. (*"Travailler c'est prier."*) The workshop for Péguy, where one works manually, is equivalent to an oratory where one prays.

Later in his life when he attempted to summarize all the lessons learned in Orléans, with the example of his mother and grandmother: catechism lessons, primary school lessons and manual work, the formula came to him quite naturally in the few words: *"c'était rigou-*

reusement l'ancienne France." Orléans was for Péguy the microcosmic greatness and reality of France.

The beginnings of Péguy are closely bound up with his discovery of France and his conviction of having once in his life seen the authentic people of France. Later, when faced with disturbing political and moral problems, he regretted the disappearance of this people. "*Il n'y a plus de peuple,*" he said. "Everyone has become a bourgeois." And then he found an astonishing explanation for this change of social status. "Everyone is a bourgeois," he tells us, "because everyone reads his newspaper." (*"Tout le monde est bourgeois puisque tout le monde lit son journal."*)

During his childhood Péguy lived close to the people. He came from them and was nourished on the grief-stricken patriotism of 1880. One should never forget that Péguy was a child of the Franco-Prussian War. At the age of twelve, he received from the hands of Louis Boitier, a cart-wheel maker, a volume of poetry which left upon the boy and the man an indelible imprint. It was *Les Châtiments,* written by Victor Hugo during his exile, inspired by his love for France. The reading of this book confirmed Péguy's patriotism, which directed his life until the moment when he fell for France at the battle of the Marne in 1914.

(2)

After searching some time for a suitable title to give the central part of this study on Péguy, I finally chose

the rather enigmatical word of "magic." The presence
of Péguy today is due, I believe, to a magical operation.
Throughout all his writings he is trying to understand
the meaning of magic, which is the power of changing
an object or a person and of seeing behind the material
object or the character its spiritual meaning. It is perhaps the effort to give to a human creature his eternal
meaning.

The great power of Péguy reveals him then especially
in the rôle of magician. I am thinking of the magic not
only of his vision and of his thoughts, but of the magic
of his language. Péguy's language, so monotonous at
times that it seems unable to move ahead, is his real
instrument of transformation.

His work is peopled with proper names: names of
historical characters and characters of his own period,
names of cities and abstract nouns which he personifies.
Each of these names is a symbol which represents and
testifies. Each of these names, which Péguy repeats time-
lessly as in some litany, ends by becoming aggrandized,
transformed, magnetized. Péguy's work has often appeared to me like a vast novel where historical characters from different periods speak to one another outside
any context of time and disdainful of any chronological
order. At other readings it has resembled a long, un-
interrupted poem where names of characters keep returning like images and familiar metaphors.

The names especially dear to Péguy were first those
taken from the history of France: Jeanne d'Arc, Saint
Louis and Saint Geneviève. And in close union with

these French saints, the two names of Eve and Mary, which return like the names of two sisters. Then the characters from Corneille's plays, who have a very particular significance for Péguy: Rodrigue and Chimène in *Le Cid;* Polyeucte and Pauline. And the heroines of Racine: Phèdre and Bérénice especially. When these characters of Corneille and Racine reappear on the pages of his *Cahiers,* they seem to speak in Péguy's own language. With Victor Hugo, who alone fills pages and pages, Péguy performs one of his most successful tricks of prestidigitation. Thanks to the transforming art of Péguy, Victor Hugo becomes what he should have become in reality: a very great poet and a prophetic voice of France. Péguy didn't hesitate to speak as intimately of the living as of the dead. His personal friends or well-known people of his period inhabit his *Cahiers:* Dreyfus, Bernard Lazare, Jaurès, Psichari, Halévy, Bergson. All these names intervene constantly, without announcement and almost without reason, like themes which explain and represent.

Péguy himself is one of his own characters. He speaks of himself as naturally as if he were speaking of Rodrigue or Saint Louis. We hear him as a pupil in the primary school of Orléans, as a walker with his heavy peasant step and plodding gait in Paris or in la Beauce. We hear him as a polemist and watch the several battles he waged all his life. We often see him in his shop in the Latin Quarter, where he played the triple rôle of printer, publisher and author—that is to say, Péguy as founder and director of the *Cahiers de la Quinzaine,* whose publication, like that of his own work, was never completed.

By this process of transformation, which we usually call "symbolism" and which I prefer to call in Péguy's case "magic," Péguy wished to prove that all these characters and himself are not limited by time. They are not really within time. They all issue forth from the most distant depths of time, Péguy as well as Saint Geneviève, in order to speak, to act, to discuss. They come especially, perhaps, in order to upset and worry us, to dislocate us from our daily habits.

I have never felt more directly than in the case of Péguy, the application of Mallarmé's great line, which has become so celebrated: *"Tel qu'en lui-même enfin l'Eternité le change."* ("Such as into himself eternity finally changes him.") We are watching today the transformation of Péguy-the-man into Péguy-the-artist or into Péguy-the-presence. It is the moment when a man ends by becoming mythical and when his work replaces him. There is something absolute about this transformation, and Péguy, more than most authors, himself performed the transformation. I do not wish to imply by this that the meaning of his work is fixed—we are still very far from understanding, even in our own way, the work of Péguy—but I do imply that the work has become a reality which we have to take into consideration henceforth. It means that the work has its place in the consciousness of humanity. *"Tel qu'en lui-même enfin l'Eternité le change"* applies also to all the characters evoked by Péguy, who seem to come from a very distant time in order to tell us really what they are and who they are. Péguy has God Himself speak, and at some length, in certain of his books. This is perhaps the supreme magic for a writer—to have God, who is outside of time, speak within time.

When the poet becomes himself, according to Mallarmé, that is, when he becomes eternalized through his word, he ceases being a person in the eyes of the world in order to become a mythical or legendary character. We are beginning to see today to what degree the person of Péguy was the meeting place of a man and a vocation, to what degree the person was directed by his vocation. That is to say, we are beginning to understand the profound difference between the person of a poet and the presence of a poet. All persons are inadequate at first, inadequate before the world and life and themselves. A knowledge of magic is necessary, a knowledge of certain magical tricks, in order to establish equilibrium between a person and the world.

Until now critics have particularly stressed the place occupied by Jeanne d'Arc in the thought and work of Péguy. Her importance is considerable and moving, but it seems so natural and logical that we no longer feel the need of explaining it by magic. Péguy himself was so impeccably a man of the Middle Ages, so fervent in his love for the Virgin, so attached to his memory of the people, so penetrated with sentiments of justice and greatness, that in order to speak of Jeanne d'Arc as he did, no extraordinary effort was necessary.

But the magic operated by Péguy on another heroine,

a great heroine of antiquity, Antigone, is more startling than the magic operated on Jeanne d'Arc. At the lycée, between the fifth class and the class of rhetoric, Péguy read the Hellenistic poets and never forgot any of his lessons. Although there are no long passages on Antigone in Péguy's work, her name recurs often in many of his *Cahiers*. He seems always ready to speak at length about Antigone, to devote to her one of the long panegyrics he did for so many others. But each time he mentions the name of Antigone, he hesitates as if he were not yet sufficiently prepared to analyze her rôle and example. Péguy often gives me the impression of preparing himself to evoke Antigone.

But the interventions of the Greek heroine are all the more beautiful and poignant through being brief. Jeanne is his constant and familiar heroine, whom he evokes at every moment, but Antigone is the prefiguration of Jeanne d'Arc. She represents another age, but her soul and her heroism recall the mediaeval heroine. Péguy wrote in *Clio*: "*Souvent c'est peut-être de la meilleure âme païenne que l'on fait la meilleure âme chrétienne.*" ("It is often with the best Pagan soul that you make the best Christian soul.") For a prophet like Péguy everything is in everything. Antigone prepares and announces Jeanne d'Arc, as Jeanne d'Arc recalls and reproduces Antigone. By the two souls of these heroines, Pagan antiquity and the Christian Middle Ages are joined. But in order to make Antigone comprehensible to us, in order to make out of her a modern soul, as Péguy did, more magic was needed, more magical resources, than for his transformation of Jeanne d'Arc.

What precisely does Antigone represent for Péguy? Why does she return so constantly on his pages? And why does she appear there always so veiled and so discreet?

The clearest answers to these questions are found, I believe, in a book of Péguy called *Les Suppliants Parallèles*. This book, one of the most penetrating and neglected of his works, is essentially a long study on the meaning and the implications of a single word. The word "supplication." Péguy discusses first the difference between a modern supplication and an ancient supplication. He reminds us of the shame and ignominy which, for the modern mind, adhere to the word supplication. *"Chez les modernes,"* he writes, *"une supplication est une opération d'aplatissement, une manifestation de platitude."* We have come to see in the act of supplication an operation of debasement, we have learned not to love supplication but to see in it a kind of degradation. When Péguy considers the Greek tragedies—and especially those of Sophocles—he does not find in the supplication which each of these tragedies represents, any trace of a process of degradation.

He quotes several examples of ancient supplication in which he sees the slow operation of an immense people, what he calls *"une infinie opération suppliante."* He refers to the example of a whole people prostrate at the feet of Oedipus, and the supplication of Priam at the feet of Achilles. And then he begins to tell us the difference between the one supplicated and the suppliant. In the eyes of the world, it is always the one supplicated who holds the better position. He is usually a king, or a tyrant, or a leader. He is almost inevitably a rich man, *"un homme qui a beaucoup de boeufs."* Péguy completes this description by telling us that the one supplicated is a happy man.

But Péguy's thesis is paradoxical. In this dialogue between the suppliant and the one supplicated, it is not the latter, it is rather the suppliant who holds the exalted position. What are the various rôles destined to the suppliant? He may be a beggar, or blind, or an exile. He is perhaps a prisoner or a victim or a child banished from his family. But always for Péguy the suppliant has the nobler rôle. He holds the first part in the dialogue. The suppliant is in reality the master.

Péguy examines for us the case of Oedipus. Oedipus began as a king. He was first the one supplicated when the people bowed themselves at his feet. But Oedipus, according to Péguy, was promoted and changed his rank. He mounted because he ended his life in the rôle of suppliant. Oedipus is noble when he appears for the first time at the moment when the people supplicate him. But he is still nobler at the end of the tragedy when he goes off as a blind man. Oedipus entered as a king and left as a suppliant.

At the end of this long passage on Oedipus and on his greatness as a suppliant, a very short note on Antigone announces another passage which is not written. Péguy, one of the most verbose of authors, also leaves blank spaces on his page, just like Rimbaud and Mallarmé, who seem to be venerated today especially for the things they did not say. One of the characteristics of modern criticism is to interpret the margins and the blank pages of an author. In the passage on Oedipus, Péguy ends with the name of Antigone. He writes: *"Oedipe sortait suppliant, et l'éternel père d'Antigone . . . L'Antigone de l'ensevelissement du Polynice fraternel."* Then comes a blank. Everything is prepared for a magnificent passage on Antigone, but it is not written. Péguy stopped just after beginning.

What is greatest in antiquity for Péguy is the ancient hero: Oedipus, Achilles, Hector. And after speaking of the greatest of the ancient heroes, of Oedipus his favorite, who began as a man supplicated and who ended as a suppliant, Péguy commenced to speak of the daughter of Oedipus, of Antigone, who was destined to make one of the most heart-rending supplications of all time.

Antigone was one of those creatures of men who are born and grow up innocent and who bear in themselves all the ancestral tares and who die for them. Péguy was drawn to Antigone because in one single day she fulfilled her destiny. The story is familiar. Antigone threw some earth over the body of her brother Polynices, which was exposed outside the walls of the city. Creon the king tried to save her because she was betrothed to his son. But the social order demanded that one of the two brothers be held as a symbol of revolt. Antigone refused not to honor the body of her brother. She was refractory.

She persisted in her refusal because she was obeying divine laws. Antigone opposed the law of men, the written law, while saying that there are unwritten laws not of today nor of yesterday, which are eternal laws. And she accepted death for having preserved her brother's honor.

This is the example of ancient heroism which Péguy loved. And we begin to see the magic by means of which he was speaking of himself while speaking of Antigone. Because Péguy was as inflexible and as courageous as Antigone. He was ready to sacrifice everything for honor, to refuse all pacts and all compromises.

The blank space which Péguy left each time he mentioned Antigone becomes more and more comprehensible. He did not need to continue with the writing and fill the space because everyone would realize that he was speaking about himself. Péguy's silence on Antigone was his modesty. For us today, in 1946, there is still a little more magic in all the passages of Péguy where it is a question of Antigone, because the example of Antigone, after serving as an example for Péguy, has served also as an example for France. Like Antigone, France sacrificed everything save honor. She almost expired in safe-guarding her pride and her dignity. Innocent as Antigone—because there is an innocent French people—she bore within herself ancestral tares of avarice, of covetousness, of a false social order. And like Antigone who descended living into her tomb, France entered a night in order to protect her purity and prepare a new destiny.

(3)

We should like to continue a bit farther with the story and the example of Antigone in France. After her apparition on the pages of Péguy, Antigone invaded the theatre. In 1922, Jean Cocteau presented in the theatre of the Atelier in Paris his adaptation of Sophocles' *Antigone*. The actor Dullin played the rôle of Creon, Cocteau himself recited the rôle of the chorus, the settings were done by Picasso, the music by Honegger and the costumes by Chanel. The première of Cocteau's *Antigone* on December 20, 1922, was an event in the modern theatre.

But during the German occupation, the theatres in Paris presented three *Antigones* almost at the same time. There was first the tragedy of Sophocles in a new translation; then there was a revival of Cocteau's *Antigone*— slightly rewritten, I believe—and thirdly, a new *Antigone* by a new dramatist, M. Jean Anouilh, performed in the same theatre of the Atelier. It appears that the Germans failed to understand this triple ardor which the Parisians felt for the character of Antigone. They failed to realize—otherwise they would have closed the theatres—the moral support which the French derived from Antigone's heroism, from the symbolism of her fidelity and her strength.

The success of Anouilh's new *Antigone,* played in modern costume, must have bewildered the Gestapo. Antigone appears in it quite rejuvenated. The play is full of intentional anachronisms. At one point in the play, for example, Antigone asks her nurse for a cup of coffee. But in reality, she is the same heroine as Sophocles', Péguy's and Cocteau's, who refuses to adapt herself to the world and whose significance was clear in the Paris of 1944.

The purity of the theme of Antigone is a miracle in the midst of the French literature of these last few years, which is on the whole profoundly pessimistic. I am thinking of the work of disillusionment and bitterness of Jean-Paul Sartre, who has become recently for the younger writers a kind of literary guide and a leader such as André Gide was ten years ago. In the theatre, M. Sartre's plays, *Huis Clos* and *Les Mouches,* are contemporary successes with *Antigone.*

By contrast with the so-called existentialist theatre of Sartre, the poignant beauty of Antigone appears all the more miraculous. The same purity inhabited Péguy and gives to his work today the prestige which it is enjoying. His is a long work which deals with quite another theme than that of human passion, which seems even directed against the movement of passion. The salient feature in Péguy's work is the absence of any discussion of love as passion. I do not believe that there is in all of his volumes a single word on love considered in its passionate aspect. And this is unheard of in our Western literature, which takes its origins in a myth like Tristan and Isolde, where love is that force which prefers nothingness to the limitations of life, where love is always the love of peril and death. Péguy placed thought before love. The purity of Antigone is a magical transformation of the concept of justice. The stubbornness of Antigone, who resists the law of men, discovered in France quite recently a new prestige in the secret and magical word: Resistance.

The theme of Antigone demands a fatalistic art. An art which, rather than disturbing the artist, will disturb the spectator. Péguy and Cocteau were both caught by the mania and the magic of writing. Like a pharmacist who mixes simples (those herbs which contain curative virtues), or like a painter who mixes colors, Péguy and Cocteau mixed up proper names, like those of Antigone and Oedipus, in order to convert them into cures or masterpieces. But the three mixing processes of the pharmacist, the painter and the writer are all magical.

I am convinced that Péguy and Cocteau are the two supreme magicians of our period. Cocteau gave to one of his essays the title: *"Le mystère laïc."* And Péguy would have approved of many of his sentences. This one, for example: "One day our period will be called the age of mystery." (*"Notre époque s'appellera un jour l'époque du mystère."*) And especially the phrase: "Antigone is my saint." (*"Antigone est ma sainte."*)

There are of course tremendous differences between Péguy and Cocteau, but they appear now essentially as differences of direction. Péguy concludes at a point which is for Cocteau a point of departure. And Cocteau follows a line which brings him back to the point where Péguy had begun. When their works are juxtaposed, they seem to form a circle.

Let me explain what I mean. In Péguy's work we watch an operation of magic which is always on the verge of becoming sacred. Péguy always begins with the temporal, usually with a proper name which is of course a temporal name: Saint Geneviève, Jeanne d'Arc, Antigone, but he always concludes by operating on this name and discovering what is eternal in it. He does this with the name of his country. Each time he writes *"la France,"* he performs a magical operation, and the temporal virtue of France is transformed into an eternal virtue. In the short phrase which I quoted at the beginning of this study, where Péguy speaks of his memory of the people: *"C'était rigoureusement l'ancienne France,"* one should be able to read a transforming piety.

In Cocteau's work we watch another kind of change. If in Péguy we see the temporal always on the verge of becoming the eternal, in Cocteau we see the sacred always in the process of becoming the magical; that is, the eternal always about to become the temporal. When Cocteau shows us in his theatre an Orpheus or an Antigone, he conceals from us the mythical and eternal traits of such characters in order to show us their human and comic traits and all their tritenesses. When Cocteau, for example, uses the character Oedipus in his play *La Machine Infernale,* he does not show him as a king, but as a *voyou* and as a gigolo.

Péguy and Cocteau are two magicians who hide nothing, who are constantly confessing. They are both interested in the problem of justice. They both oppose the justice of man, the justice of the law, but for different reasons: Péguy, because he discovers the eternal in the temporal; Cocteau, because he discovers the temporal in the eternal. In his *Lettre à Jacques Maritain,* Cocteau writes: "My instinct always urges me to go against the law. That is the secret reason why I translated *Antigone*." ("*L'instinct me pousse toujours contre la loi. C'est la raison secrète pour laquelle j'ai traduit Antigone*.")

We think of Charles Péguy as being that man who walks over the face of the earth, over the earth of his ancestors the winegrowers and the woodchoppers. Péguy incarnates the people and the fidelity of the people toward the land. And he finds in the symbol of the land and its faithfulness the sign of the eternal. We think of Jean Cocteau as being that man who walks along a tight-rope, along the tight-rope of a circus where a vast public is watching him. Cocteau incarnates the clown and the inconstancy of the public toward him. A clown on the tight-rope imitates the gestures of an angel, but when he falls into the net, he becomes a clown. In the eternal Cocteau discovers the temporal.

Péguy considers and studies ideas as Cocteau considers and studies the arts. The idea of the Greek heroine, Antigone, reveals to Péguy an entire aspect of the eternal. The art of the Greek hero, Oedipus, and of the infernal machine of the gods, reveals to Cocteau a half-concealed aspect of human psychology.

Péguy praised the Greek heroes, whereas Cocteau and the painter Chirico depicted a rejuvenation of ancient Greece. In the plays of Cocteau and in the canvases of Chirico, where there are so many walls and shadows, so many arcades and equestrian statues, we can see to what astonishing extent they have operated on Greece and rejuvenated her.

The world has its own form, but the spirit of man is constantly transforming it. Péguy transformed France, and Cocteau transformed Greece. Each country represents a certain kind of law. But when the law is made and written down, it often happens that it becomes stabilized and dies. Then it is necessary for someone to be born who will give back life to the law. This man is often a prophet. He is sometimes a poet. Péguy united in himself the two rôles of poet and prophet, of the man who first in modern France gave back life to the law.

Péguy dreamed for France and for humanity extraordinary dreams which still trouble the dreams of those of us who are living today. We know how seriously, from the age of twelve on, he took everything. He did not fail to take his dreams seriously. Today we hear a great deal about two major theories of dreams. The first says that the dreams of a man reveal solely his own secrets. This theory is largely due to Freud. The second says that the dreams of a single man reveal much more than his own secrets, that they reveal a higher world, a supra-terrestrial domain. This second theory is due especially to the psychologist Jung. In his dreams, which are his books, Péguy, like Jung, preached his conviction that the modern world must surpass the century of positivistic science, and that the modern spirit will give back life to the law as soon as it dare call the magic of its art and of its dreams by its true name of mysticism.

II · Rouault

THE ART OF A PAINTER

ROUAULT:

The Art of a Painter

(1)

THE POSITION of Georges Rouault among contemporary painters, both in Europe and in America where his work is better known and admired each year, is singularly individualistic and isolated. His canvases are, I believe, the only ones being painted today which reveal a deeply penetrating moral preoccupation. It would be more accurate to say a religious preoccupation. This fact is of course additional to Rouault's unquestioned modernism in technique: he is one of the revolutionary masters of the new painting.

But art critics have constantly employed the word "mediaeval" in speaking of Rouault. He has called himself a man of the Middle Ages. In appearing to himself and to so many others much more comparable to a mediaeval artisan than to a modern artist, Rouault raises the problem of the religious artist and the problem of the relationship between religion and art in our day.

The nineteenth and twentieth centuries in France form one of the richest periods in the history of painting. It is markedly characterized by an absence of religious works in the production of its leading painters. With the exception of Rouault. It is even possible, because of the magnitude of Rouault's work, that he is opening up a new era. Since the Renaissance there has been no art, particularly in the field of painting, which can properly be called Christian art. That is, there has been no art whose fervor and intention have served the Church, as the architecture and the sculptures of the cathedrals served the mediaeval Church. There have been isolated Christian artists since the Middle Ages, but there has been no great Christian art. With the dismemberment of Christianity, which began at the Reformation, religious art could no longer be organically united with the general life of civilization. Religious art ceased to exist when the idea of a Christian civilization in its full orthodox sense ceased to be a reality. No country today has a fully united Christian group. In one of his most recently published articles, François Mauriac writes that there are still Christians in the world, but that there is no longer a Christian people. (*"Il y a des chrétiens, il n'y a plus de peuple chrétien."*)

One of the most regrettable facts in Catholicism of the last two hundred years has been its strangely closed and even hostile attitude toward major artistic events. Recognition of the work of Rouault may help to change this. It is to be hoped that the Church, its clergy and its monastic orders, will study and accept the life work of this ardent Catholic and painter. Rouault is much more than a mere painter of religious subjects. He is a religious painter. New art, if it is great, seems destined to appear scandalous. *"La poésie est toujours un scandale,"* wrote Cocteau. But the most permanent mysteries of religion are scandalous also to the world. Whatever is great in thought and faith and in art is allied with revolution which is usually a form of rejuvenation.

(2)

The unusual circumstances surrounding Rouault's birth have often been related, and they are worth repeating for their symbolic value. He was born in Belleville, a section of Paris, number 51 rue de la Villette, on the 27th of May 1871, at the time of the Commune. It happened to be the very day that Belleville fell into the hands of the Versaillais. When the shells began falling on the house occupied by the Rouaults, Mme. Rouault was carried to the cellar, where without water, without light, and in the tumult of bursting bombs, she gave birth to her son. This event seems to predict the darkness and fury of the painter's work. When Rouault becomes a more legendary figure than he is today, when he grows into the full stature of his greatness, the violent scene of his birth will be closely related to the violence of his art.

As a boy Rouault worked from seven in the morning to seven at night in the studio of Hirsch, a stained-glass

worker, who made the windows of Saint-Séverin during
the time when Rouault was his apprentice. By eighteen
he had decided to give up the trade of glass-making to
become a painter, and entered the studio of Elie
Delaunay. This first teacher was succeeded almost
immediately by Gustave Moreau, under whose direction Rouault studied for seven or eight years. This train-
ing was conventional and academic. It is remarkable
how little Rouault reflects the painting of his master.
Moreau and Rouault represent two opposing civiliza-
tions in painting. Moreau's art is decorative, detailed
and clear; Rouault's is a work of the spirit rather than
a work of decoration, a work of broad dramatic effect
rather than one of minute detail. Moreau's reputation
in his own time seems to us today ill-deserved, and
Rouault's cult of his master is inexplicable in terms of
artistic values. Rouault still occupies the post of curator
of the museum of Gustave Moreau, and talks about his
master with extraordinary fidelity and affection. When
questioned about his own paintings, he seldom answers
directly but turns the conversation to topics concerning
Moreau.

Rouault's entire life has been spent in Paris with the
exception of a few years in Versailles before the First
World War. There seems to have been only one period
in his life of extreme personal suffering: the years immediately following Moreau's death in 1897. They were
years of solitude and nervous exhaustion. He felt then
bereft and guideless. In fact he explains the genesis of
his paintings of horror and tragedy by the personal

psychic drama he was involved in. He has said himself about this period that he began to produce paintings of an outrageous lyricism. (*"Je me mis à faire une peinture d'un lyrisme outrageant."*)

After a brief convalescence spent in Evian in 1902, Rouault returned to Paris, where he married and began a life of much greater calm than he had known heretofore. His life appears obscure and his relations with the world timid when contrasted with his work.

Art historians have already classified Rouault with a group of painters in Paris who are usually referred to by the ominous-sounding word *"les fauves."* This group includes the two celebrated students of Gustave Moreau: Henri Matisse and Georges Rouault, as well as Derain and Vlaminck. They were all rebellious against academism in art, and independent by nature. They all felt the need of returning to a kind of primitivism in expression, where in a new freedom of creation they might capture a more popular accent and tone. They were men who preferred surrealism to realism. In 1904 Vlaminck instituted in Paris the fashion of negro sculpturing, which continued strongly for ten years and influenced to a marked degree such a painter as Picasso. But there is almost no trace of negro art in the paintings of Rouault. His primitivism was something else, more closely akin perhaps to the stylized solidity of romanesque sculpturing.

By the time of the Salon exhibition in Paris of 1906, these painters, called *"les fauves,"* constituted a real force in the artistic life of the French capital. The two major schools of painting before them, the Barbizon school and impressionism, had pretty well succeeded in eliminating any specific subject matter from painting. Landscapes or apples were sufficient subject matter for a painter like Cézanne, for example. This denial or reduction of the importance of subject matter was a major step in the aesthetic revolution called "pure painting." Cubism, where there is no narrative subject matter, marks the highest point of development in this revolution. Each painter seemed to hold tenaciously to one very simplified subject, which was in fact more a theme than a subject: Utrillo chose a street scene; Vlaminck, a landscape; Modigliani, a portrait.

Only Rouault remained apart from this new aesthetic credo and gave to the various subjects he painted a meaning and reality of their own. His art certainly does not represent literalness or realism, but each picture, which is almost always of a human figure or a group of figures, is real to him in its intensity or anguish or drama. If it is true that Rouault never speaks of his own work, that is because his work is always speaking to him. The figures of Rouault are not mere abstractions or themes; they are eloquent characters whose individual and particularized suffering bears a meaning which seems to go beyond the canvas itself.

(3)

In the brief mention we made of Rouault's teacher, Gustave Moreau, we pointed out the great divergence between his art and Rouault's. One man more than any other (who was not a painter, however) seems to have formed the character of Rouault, or at least confirmed and encouraged it, and to have influenced by his own example the art of Rouault. This man was the writer Léon Bloy, a vehement Catholic temperament whose importance is being more and more recognized. Bloy was twenty-five years older than Rouault. His violent rages and his catastrophic lyricism give him a position in the field of letters not dissimilar to the position which Rouault occupies in painting. He was a kind of older spiritual brother to Rouault, who met him just after recovering from his painful period of illness. Bloy notes in his journal under April 1904 that he had definitely annexed as a friend the painter Georges Rouault.

At the beginning of this friendship, Bloy believes ardently in the talent of his young friend. But as early as November of this same year, 1904, an entry in his journal reveals the fact that he no longer understands the new sketches and paintings of Rouault. Brief notations throughout the entries of 1905 prove that Bloy was becoming more and more troubled over what he considered the atrocious caricature of Rouault's new work. It is curious that a man whose own art was cataclysmic and sombre was unable to comprehend or accept quite a comparable art in another medium. Rouault himself must have been pained by this lack of comprehension. Friendship continued between the two men until Léon Bloy's death in 1917, but Rouault remained silent during all discussions of painting.

I have often felt that the exaggerated metaphors and resounding periods of Léon Bloy are reflected in the dark frenzy which covers all the canvases of Rouault. They are two artists who extol and exploit the same hyperbole: man's despair and ignominy in the presence of the absolute. The hero of Bloy's first novel, *Le Désespéré,* he calls Marchenoir, who is of course himself, and the same hero returns in Bloy's second novel, *La Femme Pauvre.* The portrait he gives of this character, who is himself, has all the intensity and tragic foreboding which stand out in the innumerable studies of Rouault's clowns, many of whom have the painter's own face. Tragic artists like Bloy and Rouault, like Baudelaire and Dostoievsky, are so steadily concentrated on their own drama and know themselves in such abysses of their subconsciousness, that whenever they describe a character in their writing or in their painting, the features turn out inevitably to be their own. Such an artist may well appear to be a supreme example of egocentrism. But there is an awesomeness in this self-knowledge and self-portraiture of Bloy and Rouault which preserves their work from any vapid egotism.

By their style Rouault and Bloy are very close to one another. Their work is explosive, but the hyperbole of its expression does not conceal the spiritual depths from which it rises. And by their themes also Rouault and Bloy are united. The doctrine of redemption through suffering blazes forth from the books and the paintings of these two men. The one who suffers testifies to God, as Bloy says in his sentence: *"Vous souffrez. Donc, vous représentez Dieu."* Side by side are developed in these works the two themes of compassion and ferociousness, of tenderness and malediction. Rémy de Gourmont once described the books of Bloy as being the collaboration between Saint Thomas Aquinas and Gargantua. (*"Ses livres ont l'air d'avoir été écrits par saint Thomas d'Aquin en collaboration avec Gargantua."*) There is some truth in this humorous statement, because the work of both Bloy and Rouault contains an earthiness, a kind of Rabelaisian realism, as well as a spirituality which gives to the earthiness its relief and contour. These artists are Christians in revolt against the tepid society in which they see the religious mysteries neglected or misunderstood. And like all men who wage such a battle against the indifference of their age, they are solitary. Bloy and Rouault know the solitude of men who give to the world, and take very little from it.

(4)

I should like to be able to explain the faith of Rouault by the very subjects he paints, subjects which often shock and puzzle the religiously minded. And likewise, I should wish to be able to explain the intensity of his paintings by the intensity of his faith. There is only one problem for Rouault the painter, and, when all is said, there is only one problem for believers of the Christian faith. These form the same problem which is that of salvation. There were many mysteries for mankind prior to the Christian era, and some of them still exist today. But their force is less marked. It would appear that the mystery of salvation has been substituted for all other mysteries. It almost seems to be a game which Rouault depicts in his paintings, the game between human nature on one side and grace on the other. He seizes on the drama of this game as other painters seem to seize on some aspect of either human nature or grace. Rouault, in his humility as a believer, does not pretend to understand this mystery. He is rather the servant of the mystery. By painting it, he serves a force which he doesn't comprehend. In fact, every kind of creative artist serves a force or a mystery which is beyond his powers of comprehension. As soon as an artist understands the subject he works with, he ceases being an artist and becomes something else: a prophet, a scientist, a philosopher.

In the very center of this mystery of salvation, serving both as its historicity and its mystical reality, stands the Crucifixion. It is one of Rouault's subjects, and it explains in its literal Christian meaning the reason for the daily renewed struggle between nature and grace in the life of all men. The fact of the Crucifixion prevents any purely human tranquility and peace. Greek art was able to give to the world the representation of completed peace and perfection in the sculptured beauty of a Hermes and an Artemis. Christian perfection cannot be represented as something completed or mastered. It is the opposite of that, because it is always perfection envisaged as a striving, as man's effort to reach the absolute. A whole aspect of Christian art, having its source in a Jansenistic, rigorous faith like that of Rouault, depicts the anguish of the human spirit in its struggle against temptation.

Compared to Greek art, the world of Rouault is ugliness. But the real subject of his paintings is the struggle which takes place in the midst of ugliness against all the crimes of life accumulated there. In his depiction of ugliness, Rouault attaches himself to a long tradition of the nineteenth century. Goya, Daumier and Toulouse-Lautrec in painting, and Baudelaire and Rimbaud in poetry, are all examples of artists who see humanity suffused in a nocturnal and even infernal glow. What is especially distinctive in Rouault and in Baudelaire is the religion they are able to give to their theme of sordidness and sin. They are artists for whom the world of the spirit is attained through the material world, through the closed, confining world of matter. Landscapes, brothels, theatres, circus tents and seats of judges enclose the humanity of Rouault and force each character to such inner reflection that they arrive at the very frontier of hope itself. These enclosed settings of Rouault, his brothels and tents, are like the cell of a monk, where concentration has a spiritual value. The religious needs to have with regard to his faith the same kind of knowledge which the fish has of the ocean. It must become his element, surrounding him and permeating him. The faces of Rouault's characters all testify to an intimate knowledge of their atmosphere and their crime, so intimate that it has the oneness of a spiritual experience.

Rouault himself was terrified at what he painted. *"C'est effrayant ce que je fais,"* he once said. This same reaction of the artist horrified at what he has done is told about Balzac, who was unable to reread his own stories. François Mauriac has recorded how, as soon as a character is created in any of his novels, he begins to live by his own life, almost independent of the novelist. Mauriac relates how his characters resist him and defeat him finally in leading a life which he himself had not designed for them. This is perhaps a modern illustration of the old myth of Pygmalion, who fell in love with his own statue, Galatea, thereby forcing it to come to life. A strange power seems to direct an artist like Rouault (and these other men whom we have mentioned: Balzac, Bloy, Mauriac) toward a subject which first they choose, and which ends mysteriously by choosing them. It is a remarkable moment in the creation of art when the artist participates in the very suffering which he is describing. Our Lord in His life on earth was always drawn to the center of various forms of human suffering: to Pharisees, money-changers, adulteresses, fishermen who had made no catch. There, in the center of crime and suffering, He came upon a fresh seizure of humanity, a new poignancy and hope of humanity. The series of prostitutes painted by Rouault in 1905–07 are not studies in simian distortions. They are humble studies of the eternal face of man searching for God.

The two struggles of Rouault the painter which are visible in his work, the one with psychological values, the other with plastic values, are so closely joined that they appear as one. A struggle with form as if form were a person. The Biblical counterpart of this artist's struggle is perhaps in the story of Jacob, who wrestled all night long with the angel of the Lord in order to extract his blessing. When morning came, Jacob received the blessing, but the strenuous effort had maimed his body. He was to bear henceforth on his body the mark of his struggle with the Almighty. An artist like Rouault can't plunge into such mysteries of man and God without receiving their mark. Paintings of the Crucifixion and the tragic face of clowns are like the stigmata of a Saint Francis. An artist contemplates a mystery only to find that it has pierced him.

The clown of Rouault, painted so often with deep accents of shadow as if done with a thick water-color brush, has standing behind him Marchenoir, the sombre character of Léon Bloy, who moved through all excesses of evil and despair before knowing redemption. And immediately behind Marchenoir, in genealogical order, stands the most forbidding character created in nine-teenth-century French literature: Maldoror, of all literary heroes the most tragic caricature because of his pure revolt against God. It is an interesting fact that Bloy was almost the first to recognize the importance of *Les Chants de Maldoror,* by Lautréamont, and makes it the subject of a chapter in his book *Belluaires et Porchers,* which he dedicates to Rouault! This is a strange but, I believe, explicable affiliation: Maldoror, Marchenoir and the clowns of Rouault. Maldoror is the pure example of pride in his effort to set himself up as a rival and neighboring monarch to God. Marchenoir is the mixed example of pride and humility, the hero of both violence and tenderness. And finally, the clowns of Rouault represent the pure example of humility. Their heads are bent down and their eyes are usually closed, but they remember their tragic origins in the century of Maldoror.

(5)

Rouault has not escaped the accusation directed against almost all of the modern artists: that of not participating in the activity of his age, of remaining outside movements and tendencies, of not fulfilling his civic and social duties. The romantic's symbol for this isolation was the ivory tower, first used, I believe, by Alfred de Vigny. It marks, in the history of the modern artist, the first deliberate withdrawal from society, due to the indifference and coldness which the artist felt in the public of his day. By the middle of the century, this feeling had grown in intensity to one of suspicion and hostility. Flaubert openly castigates the bourgeoisie and widens the breach between the artist and the world. Whereas the ivory tower symbol represented an aloofness of spirit, the art of the writer, in Flaubert's case, is directed as an attack against society. The symbolists, later in the century, manifested a still different form of separation from the world. The stoic indifference of Vigny and the bitter caricaturing of Flaubert were followed by the esoteric art of a Mallarmé. Incommunicability was the third act of this drama between the artist and the public, and undoubtedly the most grave. It was one matter to withdraw and level vituperations, but it became a much more serious matter when the withdrawal and the vituperations were not comprehensible.

Rouault began his career just after the height of symbolist esotericism. He, and other artists of extraordinary stature in France, born almost in the same year— Proust, Valéry, Gide, Claudel, Matisse—began their work with a deep inherited knowledge of the separateness of the artist from the world. Rouault knew that there is a comparable separateness in the life of the religious. He knew that he would be accused doubly, first as an artist, and secondly as a religious artist. But the distorted and blackened world which he has always borne within himself and has reproduced in his pictures is our own world. He didn't invent it. He has been expressing his period from the ivory tower of his studio, with the angry insults of a Flaubert against the bourgeoisie, and with his symbols of clowns and prostitutes which are infinitely less removed from life than the swans and fans of Mallarmé.

His is the religious consciousness of our age. He cannot lighten himself of the weight he carries. Like Jacob after his wrestling with the angel, Rouault limps with this world he carries about. Other men before him were called by their age *"les poètes maudits"* because of their particular vision of evil. Rouault with much more justification can be called *"le peintre maudit"* because he fulfills the eternal destiny of the artist of describing what he sees. Less religious artists than Rouault can do that also. Cézanne did. And Picasso continues to do so today. But Rouault, with his fervently religious consciousness, describes not only what he sees but the forces which are behind the spectacles he sees. There is a second subject behind the obviously named subject. It is the power with which Rouault sees his subject, the religious disquiet with which he feels his subject. He is not only a painter, but a mind which contains the terrors and nightmares of the age which most of us can't face. This painter has been so loyal to the cause of art, so loyal to the subject he paints and to the spiritual force behind the subject, that Jacques Maritain had Rouault especially in mind when he composed his book on *Art et Scolastique*.

The title of *The Wasteland* which Mr. Eliot gave to his long poem published in 1922 could easily be applied to the work of Rouault. In fact, it would not be difficult to point out similarities of aims and themes in the poem and in the paintings. Eliot and Rouault attempt to give a new form or a new ordering to an ancient myth. The poet, consciously and deliberately, and the painter, unconsciously but none the less deliberately, both recreate the myth of the land blighted by a curse, the land awaiting redemption by water. Life continues to survive on this land, but it has become so devoid of meaning that it

is quite comparable to death itself. The landscapes of
Rouault and his characters are all caught in a strange
immobility and desertion, as if they were experiencing
the aridity of death much more than the fertility of life.
Likewise in Mr. Eliot's poem, countless brief scenes, in
their absence of meaning, seem to serve as a kind of
mimicry of death: drinking coffee in the Hofgarten, a
game of chess, a typist home at tea time.

The scenes from Eliot and Rouault resemble "a heap
of broken images, where the sun beats." The phrase is
from *Ezekiel*, and Eliot uses it in the first part of *The
Wasteland*. The power of Eliot and Rouault comes from
their skilful juxtapositions. Eliot places side by side a
trite, banal scene and a profound statement. In the first
part of his poem, he evokes a picture of happy love
when he speaks of "the hyacinth girl," but follows it
with the words:

> I was neither
> Living nor dead, and I knew nothing,
> Looking into the heart of light, the silence.

In Rouault's art as a painter, he performs the same
kind of juxtapositions. The rich, vivid colors encased in
heavy black outlines give an unreal theatricality to the
clowns and the prostitutes. Their meagre souls are overcome by a grotesque artifice. They seem to be trying to
redeem their diminishing souls by the lavishness of color
alone and the decisive outline of color.

Le vieux roi of Rouault, perhaps his best-known painting of those exhibited in America, has an oriental rich-

ness and bejewelled effect which Eliot achieves at the
beginning of the second part of *The Wasteland*. With
strong echoes from Shakespeare's *Antony and Cleo-
patra*, Eliot paints a scene almost of Byzantine ornate-
ness:

> The chair she sat in, like a burnished throne,
> Glowed on the marble . . .

and farther on:

> The glitter of her jewels rose to meet it
> From satin cases poured in rich profusion . . .

But the rich setting of Eliot's queen and Rouault's king
does not deceive the artist. The meaning of life has dis-
integrated also in the very midst of wealth and beauty.
The old king looks inwardly at his own unresolved
drama, and holds in his hand the innocence of a flower.
The London pub scene which follows in Eliot his vision
of "a burnished throne" serves in the same way to point
out the deathlike quality of certain modes of living.

The wasteland of the myth, that is, the land blighted
by a curse and ruled over by a king who has been ren-
dered impotent, is described in Eliot's poem by his
allusions to Dante's limbo: "I see crowds of people,
walking round in a ring"; and to Baudelaire's Paris:
"Unreal city, under the brown fog of a winter dawn."
At the end of the poem, in the section called "What the
Thunder Said," the confusion of heroes: Christ, Parsifal,
the Fisher King, is reminiscent of the confusion of
heroes in Rouault's paintings: a king, Christ, a clown,

a judge. One thing they all have in common, these heroes of the poem and of the paintings: a life which has lost its meaning, a life which is a form of death. Almost the final line in *The Wasteland*, "These fragments I have stored against my ruins," could be applied to the works of Rouault. A fragment is lifeless because it is cut off from its whole. The image of "ruins" rightfully comes to mind in the shadow of these contemporary works of art.

(6)

The humanity which Rouault paints seems ready to capitulate. His pictures placed side by side, like the series of his lithographs, would form a vast fresco of modern tragedy. It is the same vision of humanity we find in certain of the novelists: in Joyce, Proust, Mauriac, and in two dramatists: Cocteau and Sartre. If it is not exactly the vision of Europe dying, it is at least the slowing up of life in Europe, with France as the center, always the most sensitive to feel and interpret such predictions. Yet Rouault stands apart from these artists in giving to the one theme common to them all its deeply Christian aspect. This doctrine of the last things is called by the philosophical term "eschatology." Rouault is an eschatological artist. He paints the last things because of the new rise they predict, because of the hope which can come only after despair. The idea of salvation dominates his entire work.

A character of Rouault, more than those created by

Picasso or Matisse, testifies to a psychological and even an anthropological awareness. A clown of Rouault bears much more than himself. He is not merely double or neptunian, he is multiple. He stands discovering in himself much more than he is, surprised at coming upon unsuspected depths and emotions and memories. He is an individual, but much more than a single man. All tendencies of all races are in him, and there will never be enough time to test or experience them all. Most of them are submerged below his consciousness, but Rouault paints him in a moment of great calm when he is listening and hearing for the first time words that perhaps have not been spoken for centuries.

Rouault's clown is an individual, but there is nothing pure about him. He is neither a pure saint nor a pure sinner. That is a myth which Rouault repudiates and in its place restores a Christian doctrine so eloquently expounded by Bossuet in the seventeenth century. Today Rouault in his paintings and Mauriac in his novels give the full religious import to the complex psychological drama which inhabits each man. We can be shocked by the abysses and the elevations in ourselves, by the secrets and the memories which we come upon daily in our inner life. Rouault and Mauriac both teach that everything is in each man, and in addition, the burning desire to save oneself. Each individual is a race. All racial experiences are dormant in each of us, and we never know the moment when one of those experiences is to reawaken. The miracle is that God can condemn a race in order to save an individual.

These are the qualities, both eschatological and religious, which dominate the work of Rouault. It is a work which remains suspended: in the desert, in the wasteland, in impoverishment, in sinfulness. It would seem that Rouault is telling us that there man must go first. But confidently, because no case is too desperate for God.

Rouault has made an important statement about the use of painting for him, and defines it as simply one method of forgetting life. *"La peinture n'est pour moi qu'un moyen comme un autre d'oublier la vie."* Each painting of Rouault is quite conceivably a forgetting of life when it is completed, because when he is executing it, it must represent an extraordinary concentration on life. Each hero—and once again the characters of Mauriac come to my mind in company with the characters of Rouault—is concentrated on his own experience, which is also that of his race and of his moment. This hero's destiny is of course apparent in the work of non-religious artists as well. The character Mersault in Albert Camus' novel *l'Etranger,* published in Paris in 1942, is depicted as hating his death and hating the world responsible for it. It is the part given so often in French films to the actor Jean Gabin. He inhabits the novels of Graham Greene in England and André Malraux in France, where he appears desperate and disenchanted, eager to destroy himself in revolution and warfare.

But the heroes of a painting, like the clowns of Rouault, do not move. They represent the immobile renovation of an individual, the heroes reflecting the strange, unaccountable action of thought. Unable to move from the pose in which the artist has fixed them, they are concentrated on an inner lyricism, in a way characteristic of heroes of some of the greatest modern novels: those of Kafka, Joyce, Proust, Mauriac. It is a curious fact that the only heroes of literal action in modern literature, of movement and of flight, are those created by poets: by Rimbaud, Claudel and St.-John Perse. The clowns of Rouault are meditators seemingly paralyzed in the extreme degree of their immobility. They have appropriated the function of the poet, and the poets have explored the realms of heroism and voyage.

In Paris today there is a new philosophical group, or newly defined group, which is attracting many young writers and artists. It grew into prominence during the recent years of German occupation, largely under the leadership of two writers I have already mentioned: Jean-Paul Sartre and Albert Camus. Their philosophy they call "existentialism" and themselves they call "existentialists." It is true that Camus has recently stated that he is not an existentialist in a literal sense, but he retains much in common with the group. The geographical center of the new movement seems to be the Café Flore in Paris, and the doctrinal precursors, the men whose writings serve as principal sources, are the Danish philosopher Kierkegaard and the German Heidegger.

It is too early to measure the importance of existentialism, but it may well turn out to be the basis of a new philosophical attitude. I refer to it in connection with this study on Rouault because, as always, before a philosophy is systematized, expressions of it appear in the arts. In a certain sense, which I shall attempt to point out in conclusion, the paintings of Rouault illustrate the traits of the existentialist hero more poignantly than the obvious examples of heroes in Kafka and Hemingway, and even in Sartre and Camus themselves.

The particular kind of tragedy which is so moving in the faces of Rouault's clowns is summarized more succinctly in a sentence of Kierkegaard than in any other I have been able to discover. "I am no part of a whole, I am not integrated, not included." This is the existentialist anguish, the tragedy of separateness, of an individuality cut off from society. The melancholy of Rouault's clowns and prostitutes can be explained philosophically by this concept of existence as being a feeling of dereliction and of estrangement. It is a philosophy of anxiety which seems to answer the anxiety of our day, the particular worry of young men in France and elsewhere faced with our contemporary problems of life and annihilation.

But existentialists in France have already split into two groups. The first is headed by Sartre, closer perhaps in allegiance to Heidegger than to Kierkegaard, deeply pessimistic and lacking in any religious hope. The key words of Sartre are nausea, anxiety, ennui. The key word for Camus is the word "'absurd." He and the

existentialists have often been called the "absurdists."
The other group, headed by the Catholic philosopher
Gabriel Marcel and closer doctrinally to Kierkegaard
than to Heidegger, represents the religious expression
of existentialism. Each single existence, for both groups,
accomplishes a movement of transcendence, but the
pessimistic group denies any movement of transcendence
toward God.

There are therefore two worlds of separateness, one
without hope, and one with hope. This is my final attempt, thanks to existentialist philosophy, to explain the
unique quality of Rouault's characters and the religious
aspect of his despair.

The characters of Sartre's play *Huis Clos* are signifi-
cantly enough in hell, even if hell is conceived of as a
Second-Empire furnished living room. The three characters of the play, a man and two women, can never get
out from the room. Their eyes will never be able to close
in sleep. The glaring light in the room will never
diminish or go out. They will never be able to establish
any harmony between themselves. Each existence in the
room is separate from the place itself and from the
other existences. The suffering which each undergoes,
the experience of hell, is the absurd lack of relationship
or harmony with the other individuals. *"L'enfer c'est les
autres,"* is the key phrase of explanation said by the
hero Garcin.

This play on hell is of course an allegory on life for
the existentialist Sartre.[1] But the paintings of Rouault

[1] See note 1.

are allegories on hell. They are saying that this is what
might happen for eternity, but not inevitably so. The
clowns are painted in such remarkable harmony with
one another and in such harmony with their setting that
the separateness of their existence takes on a religious
aspect. The moment of Christ's death on the cross,
which has often been painted by Rouault, is the deepest
of all existentialist moments. The moment when God
dies to Himself and to the world. But we contemplate
that mystery, in a painting of the Crucifixion, with our
knowledge of what preceded that moment and what is
to follow it. The clown hangs on the world rather than
on a cross, and there Rouault paints him as dying to it
and to himself. The clowns of Rouault are Christlike
because the moment which is to follow the one depicted
on the canvas is the chance or the possibility of salvation.

III · *Maritain*

THE MESSAGE OF A PHILOSOPHER

MARITAIN:

The Message of a Philosopher

(1)

I N 1943, in the very midst of the War, an ardent
group of friends of M. Jacques Maritain gathered
together in New York City at the Waldorf-Astoria Hotel
in order to celebrate his sixtieth birthday. I remember
being impressed, not so much by the large number of
people who attended, as by the variety of types of
people who spoke on that occasion words of homage and
felicitation. There were, among others, a woman jour-
nalist, a college president, a Jewish painter, a Catholic
priest. That day was a celebration of Maritain as friend
rather than as philosopher or teacher or writer. We
were all conscious of the extraordinary power Jacques
Maritain possesses of changing the lives of his friends,
of uniting them with him and with one another, of opening them up to his ideas, or rather to the ideas he
serves.

Early in his life, when he was a student at the Lycée
Henri IV in Paris, he formed a friendship with a boy

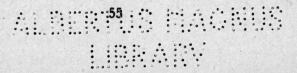

a year younger than himself. This friendship with Ernest Psichari was Maritain's earliest and, I don't believe it is exaggeration to say, his deepest. The two boys had been born into families which had distinguished themselves in the nineteenth century. Maritain was the grandson of Jules Favre, one of the founders of the Third Republic, an ardent defender of the people and of civic rights. Psichari was the grandson of Ernest Renan, the historian and writer who had early renounced his vocation of priest to become an apostle of science and rationalism. Both Maritain and Psichari came from intellectual backgrounds of liberal Protestantism and secularized humanism, a common heritage against which they both were to revolt.

They were first joined by their enthusiasm for symbolist poetry and for the movement of the Universités Populaires. Later they were joined by their conversion to the Catholic Church. Maritain made his submission in 1906 at the age of twenty-four, and his friend in 1913. Psichari had only one year in the Catholic faith before his death in August 1914, in Belgium, at the outbreak of the war. But it was an extraordinary year of spiritual grace and fervor during which he was guided and counseled by the deep friendship he had for Maritain and Maritain's young wife, Raissa. Psichari's death at the age of thirty-one gave to the young philosopher and convert a new responsibility. Maritain has had to fulfill not only his own destiny, but Psichari's as well. He has defended the faith of two men, his own and Ernest Psichari's, two faiths which stand out as revindications

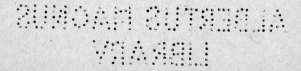

against much of nineteenth-century France in favor of both an earlier and a rejuvenated France.

I believe that the initial lesson in spirituality for Maritain was his love for the people. This love for the common man and this preoccupation with the problems of the masses lie at the basis of both Maritain's and Psichari's destiny. Together they came under the influence of Charles Péguy, became his friends, and learned from him who was the peasant (the man who had never known how to sit in an armchair) the lesson on the dignity of work and labor. Maritain introduced Péguy to his mother, Mme. Geneviève Favre, who became Péguy's best friend and guide. Every Thursday Péguy took lunch at Mme. Favre's apartment in company with Maritain and Psichari. Péguy himself was at this time moving closer and closer to Catholicism. Maritain listened to Péguy and learned much from his constant discussion of the people and the theme that no political crisis is ever separate from the religious crisis.

It is difficult to measure exactly the influences operating on a destiny like Maritain's, but after those of Psichari and Péguy, I should choose the intervention of a Semite, the lessons and the philosophy of Henri Bergson. His lectures at the Sorbonne were a great liberating force for these three men: for Péguy, Psichari and Maritain, but perhaps especially for Maritain, destined himself to become a philosopher. Bergson's attack on reason as being the one means of knowledge, opened up vast spiritual possibilities. His doctrine on intuition provided a new philosophical life opposed to the main beliefs of the nineteenth century. Bergson was Maritain's first philosopher.

One other influence on Maritain remains to be mentioned, the most violent and active of all. It was Léon Bloy who provided the necessary shock of recognition which led Maritain ultimately to his acceptance of Catholicism. In Léon Bloy he saw the Christian faith realized and lived. Bloy's faith was cataclysmic. His poverty was the sign and proof of his faith. It would seem that Maritain needed only this final example of a dedicated Christian life. He, his wife and his wife's sister were baptized on June 11, 1906, and Léon Bloy became their godfather.

Every life represents a kind of drama, and these were the characters who figured in the early part of Maritain's drama. Psichari played the rôle of friend whose interrupted life seems to us now to have been fused with the personal destiny of Maritain. Péguy played the rôle of reformer in his peasant's love of France and in his prophet's wisdom. Bergson played the rôle of teacher, and Bloy the rôle of Christian.

After his conversion, these men did not vanish from Maritain's life or cease exerting their influence. His fidelity to Psichari and Bloy is vibrant and strong even today. Differences of opinion and divergences of belief estranged him somewhat from Péguy and Bergson, but that is because soon after 1906 Maritain became the disciple of a new master. Saint Thomas Aquinas did not replace Maritain's first friends, but his philosophy taught Maritain a different rôle in life, that of a dis-

cipleship. It was a new sense or consciousness of vocation which has given all the subsequent work of Maritain
an extraordinary unity. Henceforth Maritain's will was
directed toward the reintegration of a great lesson in
France—in Paris, where Saint Thomas himself had once
taught.

Maritain has countless times referred to this dominant
function of his life. He believes that the humanism of
Aquinas, which he terms "theocentric" humanism, that
which has God at its center, was not understood in the
thirteenth century and that it is perhaps part of our own
period's destiny to rehabilitate it. Maritain has riveted
himself to one of the most dogmatic systems of thought,
not for itself, but for its possible application to the problems of today. During the last forty years, that is, during
the major portion of this century, Maritain has been
undergoing the hard, painstaking experience of disciple. Disciples may be very different from their masters:
Péguy was different from his heroines Jeanne d'Arc and
Antigone; Rouault, from his literal master, Gustave
Moreau; Claudel, from Rimbaud; but they learn from
their masters their position in the world, and they inherit
thereby a unity of experience which other men do not
possess.

(2)

Perhaps the best introduction to the work of Maritain
would be a study of his writings on aesthetics and of his
position in the general movement of modern art. His

lesson on art is not something autonomous, a kind of avocation, it is an integral part of his lesson on philosophy.

Maritain has always followed with deep understanding and passionate interest all forms of modern art. He is a personal friend of many painters, poets and musicians. The Maritains' home in Meudon, just outside of Paris, was, until the recent years of war, the gathering place of artists on Sunday afternoons. The living room was always crowded with all kinds of people: Dominicans, poets, philosophy students, dramatists, *grandes dames;* but the conversation always seemed to be about art: problems and fashions in art, the activity of artists, recent works of art. On the walls, the pictures of Severini and Chagall helped perhaps to direct the conversation in these channels.

In the writing of Maritain, especially his two principal books on aesthetics, *Art et Scolastique* and *Frontières de la Poésie,* the repertory of names of artists is vast and imposing. He seems to have neglected no school of modern art, no group no matter how esoteric. His first book on art, *Art et Scolastique,* was a discussion of the Thomistic doctrine of art. It was a difficult and courageous book to write because no specific treatise on art by a scholastic philosopher exists.

I dare say that this has reached a wider public, or at least a more diversified public, than any other book of Jacques Maritain. The success of *Art et Scolastique* may be explained, I believe, by the surprising concurrence of its doctrinal conclusions with the beliefs of modern

artists, and especially those outside any religious per-
suasion, concerning their art and their place in the contemporary world. They were pleased to see confirmed
in this work of Maritain their belief that the lesson of
art is as useful to philosophers as to artists, and that the
movement of modern art is one of the most valid and
enlightening documents on the movement of modern
ideas and modern ideologies.

Maritain's main doctrine deals with the spirituality
of art, with what might be called the transcendental or
transforming principle of art. The artist does not create
in the sense that God created the world out of nothing.
He transforms what has already been created. Art must
always belong to the category of things that are made,
of objects which are constructed, but the modern artist
has gone very far in his search for the reality of his own
being. By slightly modifying Boccaccio's phrase,
"Poetry is theology," Maritain tells us that "poetry
is ontology," because it is concerned with the science of
being. This preoccupation of the poets has pushed the
art and the function of poetry so far that it has in certain
cases gone beyond its natural frontiers into domains of
extreme danger and perversity.

Ever since the Renaissance, art has been distinguished
by its prodigality, by its waywardness and its frenzy, in
that the artist has been demanding of it much more than
it can give. He has been asking for a pure form of art,
which the philosopher might name the absolute, and
therefore a religious peace of heart, a mystical experience which art because of its very nature is incapable

of imparting. Rimbaud represents perhaps the most headstrong and violent attempt to make of poetry a deeper spiritual experience than it can be. He sought in poetry a means of changing his entire life. Rimbaud was an adolescent fascinated by the transmutation and the alchemy of the word, and his silence—he abruptly renounced writing before he was twenty years old—seems to mark an end in the apostasy of poets. His silence signifies for Maritain much more than one poet's renouncement of his vocation. Rather it is a dramatic recognition that the modern poet's quest had led him astray from the poet's goal.

But the example of Charles Baudelaire is used much more frequently than Rimbaud's by Maritain in the explanation which poetry provides him. Modern progress in the meaning of poetry begins with Baudelaire. His name dominates the period of the last eighty years of poetic endeavor and achievement, because he placed himself so very centrally in the heart of the human drama. The doctrine which Maritain refers to constantly as being the key to Baudelaire's message is that of the celebrated sonnet *Correspondances*. It is a simple doctrine, but had been forgotten or neglected for centuries. The doctrine which states that the spiritual is immanent in the real world, in what we call reality. The interchange between the material world and the spiritual world is constant, the one revealing the other, the one standing as sign of the other.

The intricate relationship which Dante establishes in

his *Divine ·Comedy* between the three worlds of the
spirit: hell, purgatory and paradise, and the one world
of matter, the one world of human life, is done for the
second time in our history by Baudelaire in his *Fleurs
du Mal*. Dante, at the end of the Middle Ages, and
Baudelaire, at the very center of the modern age, testify
to a similar belief about the work of the artist. Dante,
to his world of philosophical order, and Baudelaire, to
his world of philosophical disorder, both said that the
greatest of artistic works depends on the poet and on his
agreement with the world. Creative activity is therefore
the release or the liberating of a spiritual gift of per-
ception. In the poetic work of Baudelaire, the mysteries
of the world and the mysteries of the spirit communi-
cate with one another. The world itself is the site for
the rediscovery of the spiritual origin of man. Every
part of reality which surrounds us bears some vestige
of this origin.

The "logic" of Baudelaire, Maritain sees as being
the intimate geometry of his form. The "poetry" of
Baudelaire is something else, some value infused into
the artisan's logic. Both the artist and the man stand
behind the work we call a poem. One cannot exist without the other. The logic of the form has no value if
separated from the spiritual intent of the work. A certain movement in modern art tended to make this separation, to create pure form divorced from content, and
this tendency Baudelaire castigated as dangerous and
even pernicious. Maritain repeatedly points out that

Baudelaire, more than any other poet, prevented art from destroying itself, from committing a kind of suicide.

An article first published by Baudelaire in 1852, entitled *L'Ecole Païenne* and now included in *L'Art Romantique*, is a clear statement of Baudelaire's belief that man commits an aberration when he builds his existence around art as a supreme end in itself. The greatest poets have always had something to say to man. Maritain, in this comment, has in mind such artists as Dante, Shakespeare, Racine, Baudelaire and Claudel. They are poets who become naturally and inevitably critics. The immoderate love of form ends in disorder, warned Baudelaire. *"Le goût immodéré de la forme pousse à des désordres monstrueux et inconnus."* Baudelaire's doctrine on dandyism does not confine itself to the exterior beauty and meticulousness of dress. Rather it is a deeply spiritual doctrine. *"Le dandysme confine au spiritualisme et au stoïcisme."* Dandyism represents for Baudelaire a kind of heroism, the heroism belonging to periods of decadence and transition.

Many notations throughout Maritain's writings on aesthetics deal with the novel and with the example of novelists. Here I find his thought more difficult to follow, more troubled. The remarks always seem to center about the novels of François Mauriac. At first Maritain was disturbed at what he defined as a manichean trait in Mauriac, a tendency to equate the forces of good and evil in man, to see, as Gide does, a work of art as a collaboration between the artist and Satan.

But as soon as the accusation was levelled, Maritain seems to have reconsidered, and in the latest notes appended to his work, expresses great admiration for Mauriac.

The novelist, more perhaps than any other type of artist, has to explore the lowest parts of the city and the lowest recesses of the heart. To understand anything about the universe of man, it is necessary to possess some knowledge about the regions of evil. The Christian paradox which becomes clear in the novels of Mauriac (and in the paintings of Rouault) is the one which says that in the very sin itself of an individual resides a mystery which is not sinful but sacred. When all is said, this little phrase: "the sacred mystery of sin" is perhaps the key to all great novels, the only single definition which can apply to all novels. A novel is not constructed, as a poem is, on a single symbol or a metaphor. It grows gradually and increases like life, like a whole humanity which has to be formed, investigated and governed. The novelist in whom Maritain is interested does not create a character outside his own experience. He follows the destiny of his creatures from within them because there he discovers himself. And there he discovers how little he knows about himself. A novel therefore should not be defined as a complicity between the novelist and the devil, but as a complicity between the novelist and the mystery of his creatures. Maritain refers especially to Dostoievsky, Mauriac and Julien Green as novelists who observe the mystery in their characters. A character is not a formula or a symbol which can be fixed for all time. He changes daily. As parts of his being become clearer and more defined, other parts sink into darkness and oblivion.

Already twenty years have passed since Maritain wrote, in January 1926, his *Réponse à Jean Cocteau*. This, with the work it answers, *Lettre à Jacques Maritain*, form two treatises, or rather one treatise in two parts by two authors, which appears to us a work of great value because it is a synthesis of Maritain's thoughts about art. The case of Cocteau is significant enough for Maritain to give to him more space in his writings than to any other single artist. He addresses Cocteau by name, but through him, all other artists as well, and speaks with the authority of a philosopher who understands the position of art in the hierarchy of human activities, and with the humility of a thinker who accepts the final mystery of art.

At the very beginning of the *Réponse,* Maritain writes of Cocteau's constant preoccupation with angels. *"Toujours vous avez eu souci des Anges."* It is true that the work of Cocteau seems to transpire within a supernatural kingdom. In his film, *Sang d'un Poète,* there is a black angel. In his plays certain characters have an other-world sense: Tirésias, for example, in *La Machine Infernale*. In his essays and poetry there are allusions to angels or angelic activities which often turn out to be traps set to catch the poet. It is curious that whenever Maritain refers to angels, it seems to be in relation to two very different writers: Descartes and Jean Cocteau! Descartes he accuses of angelism, a favorite word of

Maritain, not in very current philosophical use, which seems to mean an usurping on the part of man of angelic prerogatives. Descarte's dependence on pure reason equates him with an angel. His heresy is the turning of man into an angel, and Cocteau's heresy seems to be just the opposite: the converting of an angel into a man. It is difficult to know whether the characters in some of Cocteau's plays are angelic or human. They seem to move unimpeded from one realm to another. Angels are somehow involved therefore in the two heresies which Descartes and Cocteau represent for Maritain. The first, Descartes', might be called the heresy of science, or the attempt to know by pure reason. The second, Cocteau's, might be called the heresy of art, or the attempt to know by the magical capture of the supernatural.

For some time before this exchange of correspondence, Maritain had been following Cocteau's case and the various transformations he had undergone as poet. The philosopher had been struck by the poet's familiarity with angels, but also by the number of deep-sea divers inhabiting his verse. I suppose that the angels in Cocteau are men out of their element on the earth, and his deep-sea divers are men out of their element in the sea. This study of Cocteau was especially for Maritain a joining of two lessons on art, a discovery that the scholastic theory of art was not unlike the aesthetics of the tight-rope. Cocteau's art appeared to the philosopher as one opposed to the redundant, vapid writings of the period which were being referred to as "literature." The same dichotomy was taking place in music. Cocteau was among the first to deplore the music of Wagner and to extol another kind of music represented in the work of Satie and Stravinsky. Maritain was drawn to the art of Cocteau and Satie because it follows laws of purification and simplicity, of what he would call in French *"une loi de dépouillement."*

All of these literary artists who have been so constantly admired and studied by Maritain, the poets like Baudelaire and Rimbaud, the novelists like Bloy and Mauriac, the dramatist Cocteau, have one major theme or one approach in common. It is the mystery of sin, which is vastly different from the treatment of sin itself in literature. The incomprehensibleness of sin is the preoccupation of these new artists and distinguishes them from the traditional writer. Their art does not paint Christ directly, but it is profoundly religious. They are artists who visit the lowest dives of mankind, not in order to make a lurid journalistic reporting, but to discover there the universal principle of man's hope and desire for God. The lives as well as the literary exercises of these artists are tragic for Maritain. He watches them on their tight-rope in the glare of the circus and learns from their acrobatics and their courage some aspects of the meaning of our whole civilization.

(3)

The first part of this study was a thoroughly inadequate discussion of Jacques Maritain in the rôle of a convert. Necessarily inadequate because such an experience is so private and so unknowable. He described his conversion once himself when he said that God turned him inside out as if he were a glove. Then, in the second part, we tried to explain at greater length Maritain's rôle of art critic, or rather his philosophical preoccupation with the modern artist as being the microcosmic center of our problems, as the testimonial to what is most secret and vital to the world. We come now to the third and last part of our study, which we can only touch on lightly because it is so complex and involved, so dependent on time and change. It is the philosopher's relationship with the world, Maritain's concern with the people of France, where he continues and develops the work of the prophet Péguy, and secondly, his concern with the peoples of the world, where he stresses the universality of the Catholic philosopher.

There are few great religious thinkers in our time. Maritain appears more sensitive than the others to the disorder of the modern spirit because he is so close in temperament and understanding to the artists. A great artist like Rouault reveals the malady of the modern spirit, and a philosopher like Maritain seeks to cure it. The cure can begin only after there is awareness, diagnosis and comprehension of disorder. The work of the artist is that of distinguishing and revealing. The function of the philosopher adds to the verb "distinguish" the verb "unite." This is the title of one of Maritain's books, "To distinguish in order to unite" (*Distinguer pour unir*).

In Thomism Maritain discovered a philosophical system which unites progress and tradition. His action in the world has been that of a Thomistic philosopher ardently concerned with the political and moral problems of his age and bent upon solving them in the light of the perennial philosophy, of Revelation, and the major assumptions of the Christian tradition. The career of Maritain is the drama of a philosopher in the world, of a mind moving and acting in the world. He has been involved in every aspect of the religious movement in France of the last forty years, the period which begins with his conversion in 1906 and which finds him today in 1946 ambassador of the French government in the Vatican.

The general position which Maritain has been trying to define during all this period, and always in terms of the political changes and wars which have occurred, is that of the Christian in his relationship with the world. The Christian must not sell himself to the world or give his soul to the world, but he must go into the world, speak to it, and be in it. The Christian must be in the very heart of the world, in the deepest part of the world's problems. Maritain has always taught that one can be in the center of world revolution and still maintain the independence of one's faith and one's supernatural life.

During the twenties Maritain published his main texts on aesthetics, and during the thirties he began publishing his first texts on temporal problems largely because of the civil war in Spain. Even at that time, in the middle of the decade, in 1935 when he published his *Lettre sur l'Indépendance,* the political world seemed to be dividing itself into the left wing and the right. During these last ten years of violence and tragedy and victory which may be a false victory, the cleavage is all the more marked. There are two ideologies today, the left and the right. Both express extreme views on man in his economic and spiritual life, and I do not believe that Maritain adheres to either party, any more now in 1946 than he did in 1935 when he wrote his *Lettre sur l'Indépendance.* His voice has often been heard under the auspices of left-wing groups and publications, but Maritain will speak and write wherever it is possible for him to express uncensored his views as a Christian philosopher. In fact, I think he prefers to appear in the left-wing press because there purely Christian voices are rarely heard, or have been rarely listened to until the present time.

Maritain has castigated the extreme view of both right-wing and left-wing ideologies. In its extreme, the right-wing position seems to hate justice and charity, and prefer to those principles injustice and disorder. For Maritain, Nietzsche represents a pure type of right-wing thinker whose philosophy is ultimately pure cynicism. Likewise, in its extreme, the left-wing position seems to hate the individual and sacred being of man. For Maritain, Tolstoi represents a pure type of left-wing thinker, whose philosophy is ultimately pure idealism in the metaphysical sense.

The question which Maritain ceaselessly propounds

is this: can a Christian politics, authentically and vitally
Christian, arise at this moment in history? The masses
in Europe have turned away from Christianity because
for them it has become associated with a temporal
régime which has extirpated from itself Christian truths
and practices. Some of the most inspired passages of
Maritain's writings are those dealing with the masses,
with the working and peasant classes. He sees in them
deep reserves of charity and heroism, even if they are
no longer practising Christians. Their virtues are work
and poverty. Maritain finds in them greater spiritual
values than in many nominal Christians of other social
ranks. He was dismayed at a performance of *Coriolanus*
in Paris, in 1934, I believe, when the spectators thun-
dered their approval at the insults heaped upon the
crowd in the play and thereby revealed their own
spiritual dryness.

The word on which Maritain has centered many of
his lessons is humanism. The new humanism which he
preaches would be nothing less than a renewal of civilization. It represents what he believes the world expects
from a Christian conscience and a reintegration of
Christian principles. The classical form of humanism
which has dominated the European mind ever since the
Renaissance has been for Maritain a negation of what
is deepest in man's heritage. He has defined it as being
a refusal of the supernatural in man, as a separation of
man from God. He calls it anthropocentric humanism,
in which human nature is found to be sufficient unto itself. The new humanism would be, on the contrary,

theocentric. In this philosophy, man would not be a center to himself. He would be a center opening out unto the world of the divine and the supra-rational. He would be at once a natural being and a supernatural being.

At the beginning of the year 1939, the end of which saw the outbreak of the war, Maritain gave in Paris in the Théatre Marigny a lecture entitled *Le Crépuscule de la Civilisation.* In it he states that the problem of the masses is the central problem for our period. The first solution which has been offered to this problem is the totalitarian solution in its three aspects: communistic, fascistic and nazist. Today, as a result of the war, these three aspects have become one, which was historically the initial solution: communistic totalitarianism. Maritain sees in the basic principle of communism an anti-Christian force and in the working out of its program an effort to make of the masses illusioned and standardized instruments for socialistic techniques.

The only other possible solution to this problem of the masses today he sees as being a form of Christian humanism which must begin with a revival of religious consciousness. Modern dualism has separated the things of God from the things of the world and has well-nigh made them incoherent or unmanageable together.

A novelist like Kafka and a painter like Rouault both illustrate what Maritain describes as being the defect of the modern spirit. It seems to be a form of uneasiness, a sentiment of estrangement and unfamiliarity with its environment. The spiritual danger of modernism or of the modern temperament is a dryness of heart and a certain self-love. The so-called modern critical spirit tends to become a reflexive spirit which practises not a criticism of ideas or a self-criticism, but a turning back on oneself. The modern form of solitude as we see it in the novels of Kafka and the paintings of Rouault, lacks the sense of discipline which religious solitude possesses. Maritain has pointed out many times that the notion of a Church, of religious belief, prevents sentimentality in one's inner life. The solitude which has a discipline, in the religious sense, is almost, if not exactly, a death of self in order to find God.

For the reflexive spirit, so characteristic of the modern temperament, Maritain would substitute the spirit of belief, which may best be defined as a liberating in oneself of what is indestructible. (The reflexive spirit, on the contrary, liberates in oneself what is destructible and destructive.) To define more precisely this term "belief"—and Kafka states this in his *Journal*—one could say that to believe is equivalent to being indestructible, or even, in the fullest metaphysical sense, to believe is the same as to be.

We have already written, at some length, of the supplication theme as it is analyzed in the work of Péguy. He recalls for us the example in Homer of Priam's supplication before Achilles and the example in Sophocles of the people's supplication before Oedipus. It has often occurred to me that the writings of Jacques Maritain represent one of the most moving supplications of our day.

We agree with Péguy that the suppliant has a nobler rôle than the one supplicated. Maritain is the real master today, because he is the suppliant who speaks a nobler language, a master language which comes from a great distance, from a very different place and which does not resemble the other languages we hear.

Maritain's language has the strangeness which Péguy's language has, although one is lyric and the other is philosophical. Péguy's writings might almost be considered the lyric preparation for Maritain's metaphysics. Péguy tells us, in a remarkable passage (*Bar-Cochebas, Cahier du 3 février 1907*), that philosophies are languages of creation. The Creation itself of the universe is a language of God in which He speaks to his creatures, and the great metaphysical philosophies are answers to this Creation. Platonic and Plotinian philosophies came at their time, and nothing could replace them in the history of man. This is true also for the thought of Descartes, of Kant and of Bergson. A new philosopher does not seek to prove that all previous philosophers were fools. He discovers and invents a new aspect and a new reality of eternal reality. He comes in his turn to enter what Péguy calls an eternal concert. The man who today would speak of appearance and reality must speak the language of ancient Greece. He who would speak of belief in One God and of temporal justice must needs speak the language of Israel. He who would speak of the Fall and of the Redemption of man will have to speak the language of Christianity. The man who would speak of time and space, of matter and memory and of their relationship, must speak the language of Bergson.

Maritain's language, which sounds strange to men of his day—as strange as the language of other metaphysicians sounded to men of their day—must be added to the languages of creation which are answers to the first Creation. He who henceforth would speak of theocentric humanism or humanism of the Incarnation, of the hidden, reserved sacramental power of the people, of the mystery of Israel, of the meaning of Christian liberty, will have to speak the language of Maritain.

The lyric voice of Charles Péguy during the first fourteen years of our century announced certain convictions about the human dignity of each living person which the metaphysical voice of Jacques Maritain has been analyzing these last forty years. He has been trying to teach the world to love the truth which he loves. The phrase of Saint Augustine, *gaudium de veritate,* "the joy which comes from truth," has directed his wisdom. A metaphysician's language is his most prized possession. He clings to it as Jeanne d'Arc did to her voices. When everything else went dark, she could say, "*J'ai mes voix.*" Like Antigone who said, "I was born not for hate but for love," we can say of Maritain that a metaphysician is born for the creation of his language.

IV · Myths of Modern Poetry

MYTHS OF MODERN POETRY

THE LIFE of action, or even active daily life, seems very often susceptible of compromising the power of man. I mean that a life of action may lose in habitual practice its brilliance and fervor. A hero may triumph once in his life and find henceforth that it is impossible to surpass himself or even to equal himself. But active life and its immense site of the material universe is not the only source of human heroism. Another site of man, a place which we might name the lyrical universe, seems to offer fewer compromises. There grows a well-nigh indestructible power which is called the myth of man.

What is the nature of this myth? Or, more precisely, what are the divers myths which are presented to us especially consecrated and celebrated by poetry? It would perhaps be wiser not to attempt any definition and to qualify a myth by that very useful substantive, a "mystery." But modern poetry—and this is one of its most noteworthy contributions—has taught us a great deal about the process and the profundity of the myth. We believe we understand now that the myth is formed in that lyrical universe of man, in the universe which sings, where poetry incorporates life, possesses it and fecundates it. Poetry often shatters the familiar framework where habit and law direct our lives in order to open our lives up to a mythical existence.

(1)

Let us begin with the first of the myths, the one which exalts human nature the most fervently and to which we infallibly turn in order to study man. It is the myth of drama, that experience where two forces struggle in man. Drama is that immense upheaval favorable to the growth of man and the poet. It is sometimes called passion. It is also referred to as tragedy.

For the ordinary man drama is an episode in his life which he traverses. It could even be stated that he chooses his drama in order to relieve his boredom or to exalt himself. And this marks a difference between the ordinary man and the poet in what concerns this particular concept of drama. The poet does not choose his tragedy; he is tragedy itself. The function of tragedy is not to present heroes on a stage, but to create heroes, and the poet among the first.

No poet illustrates better than Charles Baudelaire the myth of drama. He who is the inexhaustible source of so many themes in modern poetry has especially fixed the attitude of the poet caught in his particularized drama. The poet's drama is inner and permanent. It does not resemble that free struggle where gestures have some chance of appearing eloquent. Throughout *Les Fleurs du Mal* we come upon the same image of man immobilized in the center of himself, incapable of getting out from his depths, his abyss or his room. Whether it is an albatross caught on the deck of a boat, or a wounded man forgotten under a heap of corpses, the form of the Baudelairian drama is always the same representation of man riveted physically to some place, the man whose spirit wishes to escape.

Once in crossing a section of Paris, Baudelaire had seen a swan, a poor bird escaped from some menagerie which had formerly occupied a corner of the city. The poignant picture he gives of the swan bathing its wings, not in the cool waters of a lake, but in the dust of the street summarizes this myth of drama where the place which he is occupying seems always on the verge of overcoming the poet:

> *Un cygne qui s'était évadé de sa cage;*
> *Et, de ses pieds palmés frottant le pavé sec,*
> *Sur le sol raboteux traînait son blanc plumage.*
> *Près d'un ruisseau sans eau la bête ouvrant le bec*
>
> *Baignait nerveusement ses ailes dans la poudre,*
> *Et disait, le coeur plein de son beau lac natal:*
> *"Eau, quand donc pleuvras-tu? quand tonneras-tu,*
> *foudre?"* [1]

[1] "A swan which had escaped from its cage,
And, with its palmed feet striking the dry pavement,
Over the uneven ground dragged its white plumage.
Near a waterless stream the bird opening its beak

"Nervously bathed its wings in the dust,
And said, its heart remembering its native lake,
'Water, when will you rain? storms, when will you thunder?'"

In this same poem, which is entitled simply *Le Cygne*, Baudelaire evokes a further image of the same drama. The swan in the dust might appear comic as well as tragic, but Baudelaire is thinking also of a heroine of antiquity, another exile whose drama, infinitely more noble and human than the swan's, represents the same suffering of separation and imprisonment. It is Andromache, widow of Hector and prisoner of Pyrrhus, who illustrates the Baudelairian drama of immobility:

> *Aussi devant ce Louvre une image m'opprime:*
> *Je pense à mon grand cygne, avec ses gestes fous,*
> *Comme les exilés, ridicule et sublime,*
> *Et rongé d'un désir sans trêve! et puis à vous,*
>
> *Andromaque, des bras d'un grand époux tombée,*
> *Vil bétail, sous la main du superbe Pyrrhus,*
> *Auprès d'un tombeau vide en extase courbée;*
> *Veuve d'Hector, hélas! et femme d'Hélénus!* [2]

This drama, reproduced so constantly by Baudelaire that it became his only drama and the modern drama par excellence, is not new with him. Dante, in his vast repertory of dramas, devoted to it one of his most striking passages in the *Inferno*. In the seventh circle where

[2] "Before the Louvre an image oppresses me.
I think of my swan, with its foolish gestures,
Like exiles, ridiculous and sublime,
And harassed with endless desire! and then of you,

"Andromache, fallen from the arms of a noble husband,
Low slave under the hand of proud Pyrrhus,
Bent in ecstasy near an empty tomb,
Widow of Hector, alas, and wife of Helenus!"

the violent are punished and where the setting is particularly sinister, we see a forest without verdure. Dante hears moans which seem to come out from the strange trunks, and he learns that the tree trunks are the suicides themselves. Since in life they had struck their bodies, in hell they are deprived of any human form. Dante breaks off a small branch and the tree cries out: *"Perchè mi scerpi?"* ("Why do you tear me?") *"Uomini fummo, ed or sem fatti sterpi."* ("We were men and are now changed into trees.")

Like the symbols of Baudelaire, his swan and Andromache, each suicide in the scene of Dante is immobilized. He has become a tree trunk inracinated in the ground. The horror comes from the fact that we do not see the character. We hear him speak, but we do not see any posture, any exterior gesture. The suicide whom Dante mutilates in breaking off a branch is Pier della Vigna, a poet of the Sicilian School and a counselor of Frederick II. Dante is so moved by pity in this encounter with a poet whom he admires and whom he discovers in hell in a form so soberly tragic, that he is unable to ask questions.

There exists a striking parallel between Baudelaire's swan, escaped from its cage and dragging its white wings through the mud of the street, and the gnarled, dried-up tree in Dante's Hell whose words are those of a poet dreaming of justifying himself in the world. In Baudelaire's poem the humble wretchedness of the swan prefigures the noble and tragic pose of Andromache exiled in the palace of Pyrrhus. In Dante's poem the grotesque trees without foliage, constantly devoured by Harpies, prefigure the involved psychological drama and portrait of the poet Pier della Vigna evoked solely by his own words.

Each of these pictures represents the same drama, and in each one we see two different aspects of the drama. Whether it appear humble or noble, this drama conceals a close identification between the poet and his symbol. The swan's drama is Baudelaire's, as the drama of Pier della Vigna, in an unquestionably far more mysterious manner, is Dante's. Baudelaire establishes a correspondence not only between himself and his wretched swan or his weeping Andromache, but between him and his reader, whom he apostrophizes in another poem : *"Hypocrite lecteur, mon semblable, mon frère."* It is by means of a very strong emotion that Dante identifies himself with Pier della Vigna. He seems to share some of the physical suffering of the suicide. He does not forget that Pier della Vigna was a poet like himself and therefore submitted to a comparable destiny. As he stands before the painful example of the tree trunk which bleeds without being able to help itself, Dante experiences the static example of hell. And as Baudelaire stands before the other painful example of the swan far from its native lake, he experiences the static atmosphere of his own nature.

The great artist welcomes all voices into himself, as Dante so faithfully reproduces the words of Pier della Vigna ; or we might even say that the great artist discovers all voices within himself, as Baudelaire recognizes himself in the imprisoned bird and in Hector's widow helpless in exile. The modern drama, as demonstrated in literature, is of an immoderate tension, due especially to Baudelaire's art. It is more bare than Dante's drama, more stripped, more limited by a single, inexorable setting. There are traces of this Baudelairian drama in the final scene of Joyce's novel *Ulysses,* where Molly Bloom dreams and thinks in her bed; in the recent French play *Huis Clos,* of Jean-Paul Sartre, where the three characters remain in a single room, and in the American film *The Lost Weekend,* where the hero locks himself up in his apartment.

(2)

The second myth of modern poetry, to which we come now in this arbitrary choice, is the myth of voyage. It is radically opposed to the myth of drama such as we defined it as being the drama of immobility or of the closed-in site. At other periods the solitude of a room or of a pose served as inspiration for the lyricism and the song of man. Voyage represented at that time his drama and his adventure. But today it seems to be just the opposite. The drama of man is now his solitude and his room, whereas the voyage has become his principal source of lyricism.

In his innumerable tales of voyage, the modern poet inflicts on the word the form of lyrical reality. He attains to his most spiritual moments, there where he is most purely spirit, in his voyage-poetry. He is able in it to revindicate an ancient rôle of visionary, of the man who sees what men don't see and who tries to lead us to the very gates of mystery. The poet must first abandon his people in order to survive as a hero. It is a significant fact that most of the great modern poets have literally left their country in order to live elsewhere. Since Rimbaud, who seems to have consecrated the flights of the poet by his own voyages to so many different countries, the world has witnessed a series of physical departures and watched poets settling under foreign skies: the Austrian Rilke in Paris, the French Claudel in Japan, the American Eliot in London, the English Auden in the United States, the French St.-John Perse in Washington.

But voyage does not solely signify departure. It is also arrival, it may mean the stopping of the poet for a time. In the first part of the poem *Anabase,* by St.-John Perse, the poet appears in the rôle of conqueror who establishes himself in a foreign land. The images of this very profound text help us to understand the myth of voyage. The word "power" (*"puissance"*) used four times on two pages has particular resonance. We first learn that power comes from the sun, but this sun is not named. Power sang on the night routes followed by the poet. It is perhaps this power which has the poet say, when he addresses the conquered people: *"J'ai dessein de vivre parmi vous."* ("I plan to live in your midst.")

Travellers are seekers. This solar power really symbolizes the life of the spirit, which is at times revealed in a form of restlessness and hunt. The first story of Adam and Eve, expelled from Eden, lies at the genesis of the life of the spirit. A fragment of *Anabase*, in which Perse names all kinds of voyagers, possesses an Eden-like tonality and evokes the first departure of man-the-seeker. In this litany of voyagers the universe also is described. The myth constructed by St.-John Perse corresponds to the image of the universe. The solar power illumines and inhabits the material world:

> *Hommes, gens de poussière et de toutes façons, gens de négoce et de loisir, gens des confins et gens d'ailleurs, ô gens de peu de poids dans la mémoire de ces lieux; gens des vallées et des plateaux et des plus hautes pentes de ce monde à l'échéance de nos rives; flaireurs de signes, de semences, et confesseurs de souffles en Ouest; suiveurs de pistes, de saisons, leveurs de campements dans le petit vent de l'aube; ô chercheurs de points d'eau sur l'écorce du monde; ô chercheurs, ô trouveurs de raisons pour s'en aller ailleurs,*
>
> *vous ne trafiquez pas d'un sel plus fort quand, au matin, dans un présage de royaumes et d'eaux mortes hautement suspendues sur les fumées du monde, les tambours de l'exil éveillent aux frontières l'éternité qui bâille sur les sables.* [1]

[1] "Men, creatures of dust and folk of divers devices, people of business and of leisure, folk of the frontiers and foreign men, O men of little weight in the memory of these lands; people from the valleys and the uplands and the highest slopes of this world to the shores' end; Seers of signs and seeds, and confessors of the western winds, trackers of beasts and of seasons, breakers of camp in the little dawn wind, seekers of water-courses over the wrinkled rind of the world, O seekers, O finders of reasons to be up and be gone,

you traffic not in a salt more strong than this, when at morning with omen of kingdoms and omen of dead waters swung high over the smokes of the world, the drums of exile waken on the marches

Eternity yawning on the sands." (Translated by T. S. Eliot.)

This sustained and ornate passage teaches us that exile (or what we too summarily call "voyage") celebrates eternity. The voyage is undertaken through physical or material means, but for a spiritual goal.

The profound meaning of voyage is therefore love. The will to depart is identical with the will to love. John Donne in one of his sermons tells us that: "The first act of the will is love, for till the will love, till it would have something, it is not a will." (*Sermon 23.*)

It is in the fourth section of *Purgatory* that Virgil speaks to Dante on love and free will. We are in the region of the "*accidiosi*," of those people who had been slow in their spiritual life and who in Purgatory expiate their negligence by running ceaselessly. The excessive movement of the spirits in this scene has a relationship with the discourse on love. Virgil profits from the forced stop, imposed by the falling night, in order to explain the nature of love. He says that love is the spiritual union of the soul with the beloved and that to accomplish this union the soul runs toward the beloved rapidly or slowly, depending on the obstacles or the absence of obstacles. This rather didactic speech of Virgil seems to prepare the scene in which the spirits of the "*accidiosi*," scarcely visible, traverse the growing night in a frantic race. Their speed is so great that they cannot even stop to speak. They cry out a few words which remain incomplete and enigmatical.

This scene of *Purgatory* creates a significant contrast between Dante, who collapses from fatigue and is on the point of falling asleep, and the spirits, who are running as in a whirlwind in order to expiate all the faster their former sloth. It illumines the myth of voyage by its picture of flight where space is devoured, time abolished, sidereal revolutions threatened. It teaches us, first by the sober lesson of Virgil, and then by the vision of fleeing spirits, that no lyricism can be static or fabricated. All lyricism on the contrary is a movement of the soul. The voyage is therefore its most primitive symbol, and the poet resembles the eternal maladjusted hero of odysseys, exoduses and crusades.

The anagogical (or spiritual) meaning of the voyage is easily revealed in these two fragments of mediaeval and modern poetry. The ardor manifested in the race of the spirits is explained by the salvation which awaits them at the end of their expiation. Purgatory is a kingdom based on the concept of progress, advance, change. The solar power of the conqueror in the poem of St.-John Perse reveals to him a premonition of kingdoms which is nothing less than eternity yawning over the sands. Modern lyricism reproduces the voyage and consecrates its myth. Dante's lyricism is more dramatic, but St.-John Perse, like his precursor Rimbaud, has tracked down language in order to exhaust its last resources of expression. He uses startling, fresh words which are not worn out, which appear like words coming from distant voyages and unknown countries.

(3)

After evoking the poet in his drama and the poet in his voyage, it is now time to consider the myth of the poet himself. In his drama and voyage we have seen him attached and free. Baudelaire's swan, ironically bathing its wings in the dust, and St.-John Perse's conqueror, who establishes his law in a new city and forms the plan of living among new peoples, illustrate the two myths by means of which we can perhaps enter upon the essential myth of the poet.

Has the tradition of modern poetry, the one which begins with the second generation of romantics, in the sonnets of Gérard de Nerval and the early poems of Baudelaire, formed or regenerated a being recognizable by his function of a poet? What is his dominant trait by which he distinguishes himself from other men of his period? I mean: distinguishes himself from his time in order to understand and write it. A true artist does not misunderstand the meaning of his period. He does not need to play the rôle of Cassandra, but he becomes nevertheless the illumined conscience of his period and of a destiny infinitely greater than his personal destiny. He writes this collective destiny and succeeds in identifying himself with his book.

In order to preserve the penetrating lucidity and the childlike impertinences so necessary for the accomplishment of this work, the poet must remain all his life the innocent in the midst of men who have lost their innocency. The myth of the poet is the myth of innocency, the parable of the innocent man who undergoes all the common experiences without thereby losing the purity of his being or of his heart.

The world has called Arthur Rimbaud by all kinds of names: *voyou,* vagabond, visionary, communist, Catholic, surrealist, adventurer, mystic. But this prodigality of rôles assigned to Rimbaud is the very proof of his innocency. He is the supreme type of the innocent. He incarnates the myth of the poet more explicitly than any other artist, and his book is so explicitly the book of the innocent that most men have not yet learned how to read it.

The entire universe acts on Rimbaud. Everything impresses him, but after each impression and each experience, he repeats to himself the magic formula of the innocent: "*la vraie vie est absente.*" This formula, which is in *Une Saison en Enfer,* applies just as well to the swan which Baudelaire saw in Paris far from its native lake, and to the conqueror of St.-John Perse who establishes himself in a city for a limited time.

The child does all that the poet does: he changes everything. His purity demands that he transform all objects and that he escape. Rimbaud speaks of his childhood and of his poet's life when he tells us in *Une Saison:*

> *J'aimais les peintures idiotes, dessus de porte, décors, toiles de saltimbanques, enseignes, enluminures populaires; la littérature démodée, latin d'église, livres érotiques sans orthographe, romans de nos aïeules, contes de fées, petits livres de l'enfance, opéras vieux, refrains niais, rythmes naïfs.*[1]

[1] "I loved maudlin paintings, decorative panels, stage-sets, the backdrops of mountebanks, old inn signs, popular prints; old-fashioned literature, church Latin, erotic books innocent of all spelling, the novels of our ancestors, fairytales, children's storybooks, antiquated operas, inane refrains and artless rhythms." (Translated by Louise Varèse.)

This is another litany, to be placed perhaps before that of *Anabase* with which we began. A litany composed of objects which the imagination of a child metamorphoses into a lyrical universe. A child has only to look at a few backdrops used by clowns or read a few fairy stories to know intensely that his "real life is absent." The signs of a tavern, the Latin of the Mass and pornographic books may serve as starting points in the life of a child for the most intense spiritual experiences. The child does not flee the universe, he magnifies it. And the poet thus creates his own myth.

The two short lines of Rimbaud:

> *Elle est retrouvée!*
> *Quoi? L'Eternité*

describe this process by which the most simple and familiar objects reveal to those who know how to see: that is, children and poets, unlimited spaces and supraterrestrial beauties. Rimbaud's poetry is a song on the theme of innocency. His profoundest work, *Les Illuminations,* is a song of love. But the love song of a child who celebrates the exuberance, the transformation and the magic of love. Rimbaud does not give us the circumstantial account of his love in *Les Illuminations,* but he describes the successive moments of an existence consecrated to the tempting of adoration.

What we have been calling the three myths of modern poetry are in reality three degrees which mount toward creation. The first, the myth of drama, synonymous with passion, and the second, the myth of voyage, synony-

mous with curiosity, appear more simple to analyze than
the third, the myth of the poet, which is that of innocency.

Rimbaud's example can hardly be separated from
Mallarmé's. And yet, they are very different! Whereas
Rimbaud illustrates the first innocency of a child, Mallarmé illustrates the rediscovered innocency of the master. They represent in a way the two poles of innocency,
Rimbaud at the beginning of life, Mallarmé at the end
of life. Rimbaud's book celebrates much more than his
life and his spirit. It overflows with visions and hallu-
cinations. But Mallarmé's book celebrates much less
than his life and his spirit. It is a distillation, a purification. His poems resemble some diminished débris of a
greater work which exists intact in another sphere.

Rimbaud is the adolescent poet, always on the road,
"far," as he says himself, "from birds, flocks and village girls" (*"loin des oiseaux, des troupeaux, des vil-
lageoises"*). But Mallarmé is the priest, the poet-cleric,
seated behind the fragments of his work, from where he
teaches a doctrine more vast and profound than the
one revealed in his book. Mallarmé is like the mediaeval
theologian who knows that the work, whatever its purity, whatever its perfection, is nothing by comparison
with truth. Thus he teaches negatively, as the mediaeval
philosophers were more adept in saying what God is not
than in explaining what He is.

Here is a brief passage of *Toast Funèbre*, by Mallarmé, in which he defines the poet's work as that which
"awakens the mystery of a name." The poet "appeases"

the beauty of creation, the beauty of Eden, by naming a rose or a lily, and this verb "appease" seems to contradict other verbs: reveal or create, for example. In the same passage Mallarmé defines the destiny of the poet, which is that of disappearing without revealing. The idea of survival is a "sombre belief" for the poet. He sings rather the light of absence:

> *Le Maître, par un oeil profond, a, sur ses pas,*
> *Apaisé de l'Eden l'inquiète merveille*
> *Dont le frisson final, dans sa voix seule, éveille*
> *Pour la Rose et le Lys, le mystère d'un nom.*
> *Est-il de ce destin rien qui demeure, non?*
> *O vous tous, oubliez une croyance sombre.*
> *Le splendide génie éternel n'a pas d'ombre.*[2]

The meaning of the last line is not very different from the meaning of Rimbaud's phrase: *"La vraie vie est absente."* Whereas Rimbaud teaches the poet to abandon life, Mallarmé teaches him to abandon the word or the poem. A poem becomes worthy of that name, for Mallarmé, when it is emptied of life and all that changes. The poet must become irresistible, as life can never be. After *"l'heure sainte des quinquets"* ("the sacred hour of lamps"), Mallarmé leaves his room and assumes the rôle of absent master. When the poet enters death, his work enters life.

[2] "The Master, with profound vision, has, over his steps,
Appeased the restless marvel of Eden
Whose last quiver, in his voice alone, awakens
For the Rose and the Lily, the mystery of a name.
Does anything remain of this destiny, no?
O all of you, forget a sombre belief.
The glorious eternal genius has no shade."

The contrast between the extraordinary part of Rimbaud's life and the perfect simplicity of Mallarmé's provides endless speculation. Rimbaud is literally *"l'homme aux semelles de vent"* ("the man with the shoes of wind") who voyages through all countries, who leaves one continent after another. Mallarmé does not travel, except to go from one lycée to another, leading always the same life of an obscure teacher shamefully salaried and trembling that he might lose the one post he feels himself capable of occupying. The image we have of Rimbaud constantly on the road in the most distant countries where no one recognizes him, where no one sees him, contradicts the image we have of Mallarmé in his apartment on the rue de Rome, receiving his friends on Tuesday evenings, smoking his favorite pipe, and remaining standing all evening, from nine to midnight.

Rimbaud, in his rôle of revolutionary and adventurer, seems very different from Mallarmé in his rôle of humiliated teacher, of misunderstood and derided poet, of insignificant bourgeois. But they are close to one another in their belief about the fate of the poet. They both spoke of the degradation and the exile of the poet, of what we have called the myth of drama and of voyage. The examples of Vigny in his ivory tower and of Hugo on his island do not appear strange to Rimbaud and Mallarmé. In the homage which Mallarmé pronounced over the tomb of Verlaine, he speaks of the *"triste honneur de l'isolement"* ("the sad honor of isolation"). One sentence especially in this speech where

Mallarmé explicitly evokes the life of Verlaine could apply to all poets. *"La solitude, le froid, l'inélégance et la pénurie . . . d'ordinaire composent le sort qu'encourt l'enfant avec son ingénue audace marchant en l'existence selon sa divinité."* ("Solitude, cold, homeliness and poverty usually compose the fate which the child undergoes with his ingenuous boldness walking in life according to his divinity.")

I like this sentence of Mallarmé, which contains of the poet the solitude of his human drama and the innocency of his spiritual drama. On the threshold of life Rimbaud the adolescent tempts his innocency, exploits it and wastes it perhaps. In *Toast Funèbre,* which celebrates the death of Gautier, Mallarmé sings of the innocence of words, an innocence retrieved by the poet in the mystery of names and in the alchemy of language.

This theme of innocency, which we are considering the essential myth of the modern poet, is apparent in the *Four Quartets* of Mr. T. S. Eliot.

The first of the Quartets, *Burnt Norton,* is a meditation on time. The setting is a rose garden, the first world of children:

> Footfalls echo in the memory
> Down the passage which we did not take
> Towards the door we never opened
> Into the rose-garden.

It is possible that this rose garden is entirely imagined, but it is nevertheless the first world of enchantment, of freshness and innocency. This state of innocency, this

vision of children inhabiting a rose garden, helps Eliot
to understand a philosophical concept of time:

> Time past and time future
> What might have been and what has been
> Point to one end, which is always present.

The child's game, like the game of poetry, tends to
abolish every frontier. It effaces all notion of the past
and future. Like the poet who, in his work, emanates the
cosmos, preserves it and destroys it.

The first Quartet, which evokes childhood, recalls
the example of Rimbaud, who at the beginning of his
life confused the order of time and of the cosmos. The
second Quartet, *East Coker,* which evokes the work of
the poet, recalls the example of Mallarmé. Time here
is explained by the mystery of history, by the dark
knowledge of the poet who, as soon as he has learned
how to use words, no longer feels the need to speak:

So here I am, in the middle way, having had twenty years—
Trying to learn to use words, and every attempt
Is a wholly new start, and a different kind of failure
Because one has only learnt to get the better of words
For the thing one no longer has to say, or the way in which
One is no longer disposed to say it.

This is the other kind of innocency which we first illus-
trated by Mallarmé's silence. The first innocency, Rimbaud's, is an upheaval and a derangement; it is the rose
garden which the poet has never seen but which he
resurrects by the gift of purity. The other innocency,

Mallarmé's, is that communion with the universe when all idea of time is abolished. That is why Eliot ends his meditation on time by an image of the sea, which has no form or limits or development:

> The wave cry, the wind cry, the vast waters
> Of the petrel and the porpoise. In my end is my beginning.

In a passage of the last Quartet, *Little Gidding,* Eliot describes himself in the rôle of an air-raid warden on his night patrol. It is the hour just before dawn. The enemy airplanes have disappeared. All is silent when suddenly the poet meets a man who seems blown toward him by the wind. Eliot believes he recognizes on the face of this stranger the features of one of his masters long since dead:

> Between three districts whence the smoke arose
> I met one walking, loitering and hurried
> As if blown towards me like the metal leaves
> Before the urban dawn wind unresisting.
> I caught the sudden look of some dead master
> Whom I had known, forgotten, half recalled
> Both one and many; in the brown baked features
> The eyes of a familiar compound ghost.

When Eliot cries out to the phantom: "What! are *you* here?" we know that behind the immediate scene of the poet in London during the war, there is another scene of poetry, a scene from Dante where the poet recognizes his former teacher Brunetto Latini and says in his grieved surprise at finding him among the damned, *"siete voi qui, ser Brunetto?"*

Eliot has a great predilection for this canto of the *Inferno* where the poet Dante meets his master. Farther on, in another circle, Dante feels the same sentiment of pity for the poet Pier della Vigna, whose spirit is imprisoned in a tree trunk. The poets succeed one another. The innocency is maintained from one work to another.

> Every phrase and every sentence is an end and a beginning,
> Every poem an epitaph.

Eliot writes thus at the end of *Little Gidding,* and Mallarmé in *Toast Funèbre* expresses the same thought. Baudelaire, who thinks of Andromache exiled far from her husband's country, reproduces the same burst of innocency which attaches the poets to one another and converts the past in a present.

We learn the myth of the poet by reading his book. The meaning of his life will always escape us. But as soon as the consciousness of the poet gives itself limits and reflects itself therein, his work is created, and his myth at the same time.

We have seen how the poets engender one another by perpetuating the same myth. Certain of their books are difficult to understand, but all the arts can help us. I have often thought that a course on modern poetry should begin, not with the poems of the real poets, but by the early films of that small man who is perhaps the most astonishingly poetic figure of our period, Charlie Chaplin of the screen. He is an authentic poet who contemplates life from an heroic angle. Chaplin illustrates all of the aspects of the myths which we have described. He often appears enclosed within a hostile place, like Baudelaire's swan, both comic and tragic. Or in the rôle of the traveller going from city to city, or from saloon to saloon, in search for the ideal. Rather than wearing the buskin or the mask in the manner of ancient actors, he has his shoes, his small round hat and his cane. His passions are our own. (*"Hypocrite lecteur, mon semblable, mon frère!"*) He juggles with them as Baudelaire and Rimbaud do.

Hart Crane evokes in one of his poems, *Chaplinesque,* the design of films which exalt this myth:

> And yet these fine collapses are not lies
> More than the pirouettes of any pliant cane;
> Our obsequies are, in a way, no enterprise.
> We can evade you, and all else but the heart:
> What blame to us if the heart live on?

Here Hart Crane, poet of poems, identifies himself with Chaplin, poet of films. They both play the same rôle of the tragi-comic buffoon.

The multiform genius of the modern poet permits him to attain to all insolences as well as to all tragedies. Even this single study has listed many masks and rôles: an impotent swan, Andromache, a gnarled tree trunk, a conqueror, an adventurer, a master, an air-raid warden, a buffoon.[3] So many costumes to clothe the same heart! Hart Crane spoke thus in his poem on Chaplin: "What blame to us if the heart live on?" The heart is the sole invulnerable theme around which the poet

[3] See note 2.

orders his thought. This modern poet is a curious Narcissus who dominates, not the mind of others, but his own. The heart is the site of his drama, the goal of his voyage and the entrance into that lyric universe where the poet allows his myth to be constructed.

Notes

The Frontispiece

GAUGUIN:

Jacob and the Angel

In 1889, Paul Gauguin was living in Brittany, at Pont-Aven. When his large painting, representing Jacob's struggle with the angel, was finished, he offered it to the village priest for his church. It was refused. Then he offered it to the church at Nizon. It was refused there also. The painting finally got into an auction in Paris and was sold for 900 francs.

Gauguin himself called his picture, *La Vision du Sermon.* The vision was evidently suggested by a sermon heard at mass. The Breton women have come out from church, and are kneeling as if they still contemplate the subject evoked by the priest's words.

The night of Jacob's struggle is in the closed eyes of the pious women. Their white coifs are more placid and more solidly massed than the outstretched wings of the angel. The world of struggle and the world of contemplation are separated by the tree. The group of Jacob and the angel is diminished and microcosmic. In one sense its action seems to be taking place at a great distance from the kneeling women, and yet in another sense, it seems to be within them, at a central point in their meditation.

I like to consider this picture of Gauguin as a symbol of the particular kind of fidelity we have studied in these essays. France is obstinately faithful to herself. The faith of the Breton peasant women would be comparable to that of the people of France. The tree which cuts across the center of the composition would be the ancient faith of the land itself, the secular memory of the earth and of the centuries. Jacob, almost overcome in his angelic combat, would be the prophet or the artist or the thinker, who, apart from his people, engages upon a contest whereby he may extract, because of his vocation of solitude, a blessing for himself and for those who watch without always seeing or understanding.

Note 1

Existentialist Theatre

(1)

The term "existentialist" as applied to a distinguished group of French writers who have been active in Paris during the last eight or nine years, was first used almost by chance, in much the same way that the word "cubist" took its origin. The writers in question objected for some time to the term, but finally, weary of opposing a fashion which had rapidly spread, accepted the name with many of its original philosophical implications. The leader, M. Jean-Paul Sartre, now edits *Les Temps Modernes,* the recognized periodical of the movement. There are essays and philosophical treatises which explain the existentialist attitude. *L'Etre et le Néant,* a 700-page work by Sartre, who was at one time a teacher of philosophy, is the most elaborate statement to date and may well be a landmark in the history of French thought. As yet, Americans have not had the opportunity of studying this major work, but a few copies of the novels and plays have reached us.

Albert Camus, who now claims that he is not an orthodox existentialist although he retains much in common with the group, Jean-Paul Sartre and Simone de Beauvoir all show great diversity in their writings. Each one of them has published essays, novels and plays. During the recent German occupation the existentialist theatre proved to be one of the most successful aspects of the movement, and it is now probable that New York will see an adaptation of Sartre's play *Huis Clos*. Their theatre is metaphysical and not psychological. The word *"existenz"* in the writings of the German philosopher Heidegger signifies the being of man, or *Dasein*. Existence is for him a progress toward annihilation or nothingness. The novels of Kafka illustrate the vain search of man's existence, his gratuitous condemnation. The forlornness of man, as described in the writings of the Danish philosopher Kierkegaard, is closely allied with the existentialist nausea toward life, with the homelessness and fearfulness of the characters created by the French writers. "I am unable to make the movements of faith, I cannot shut my eyes and plunge confidently into the absurd, for me it is an impossibility," writes Kierkegaard in his book *Fear and Trembling*.[1] Countless sentences in Sartre's novel *La Nausée* bear the same resonances and reflect the same metaphysical dilemma. *"Nous étions un tas d'existants gênés, embarrassés de nous-mêmes, nous n'avions pas la moindre raison d'être là."* [2]

(2)

Sartre's play *Huis Clos* was first performed in Paris, at the Vieux-Colombier, in May 1944. The action takes place in hell,

[1] P. 44. [2] *La Nausée,* p. 163.

represented by a living room furnished in Second Empire style. The illumination is glaring and constant. The action is never interrupted and might well continue forever after the single curtain comes down. There are three characters, a man and two women, who are introduced one after the other into the room by a kind of bell hop. The idea of hell is ingenious in its use of existentialism. For each character, hell is the presence of the other two. *"L'Enfer, c'est les autres,"* is one of the final sentences spoken by the hero, and it is substantiated by the entire action and movement of the play. The theme is the disgust which each character feels because of the contingency of existence.

Garcin, the man, is a deserter who had been shot when try-ing to escape military service. Inès, the first woman to appear, is a Lesbian who had seduced her cousin's wife. Estelle, the second woman, is an infanticide, who had killed the baby she had had by a lover. The play appears to fall into four move-ments. The first, a scene between Garcin and the bell hop, is the discovery of the room and the inquiry into the kind of punishment which awaits the newcomer. Garcin discovers one main difference between the room and life. Here he will never sleep because his eyelids are unable to close. He is struck by the constancy of the light and the absence of a mirror. The second scene begins with the appearance of Inès, who, like Garcin, is perturbed to find no looking-glass. But to this initial theme is added the feeling of irritability. Garcin's nervous twiches exasperate Inès. The third movement, beginning with Estelle's entrance, is longer than the first two. Each of the characters lies to the other two about his reason for being in hell. When they realize the uselessness of subterfuge in such a place, the fourth movement is given over to a series of con-fessions. In place of a mirror, in which they might see themselves, Estelle, during her confession, has an awareness of what is going on in the world. She literally sees a dance hall where her lover is dancing with a girl. This power of vision causes her to suffer.

Huis Clos, which observes so strictly the law of the three unities and whose style is sober and non-analytical, is an admirable development of Baudelairian drama. It is the drama of the closed room and immobility, the torture of the place from which one cannot escape. The particular kind of tragedy which is so moving in the faces of Rouault's clowns, is summarized succinctly in *Huis Clos.*

(3)

The second current success of the new theatre in Paris is *Caligula,* by Albert Camus. This play was written in 1938 and therefore antedates, I believe, Camus' essay *Mythe de Sisyphe* and his novel *L'Etranger.* It was published in 1944 and first performed in 1945.

The style of *Caligula* is very close to the traditional classical style of the French theatre. After so many paltry and unconvincing attempts at "realism" and "naturalism," this play of Camus, more perhaps than his other play, *Le Malentendu,* represents a means to recapture and re-animate a great tradition. Its language has traits of purity and forcefulness which were developed in the seventeenth century and which reappeared in the twentieth century, first in the theatre of Jean Cocteau. It is true that there are themes and tonalities of lyricism, cruelty, impertinence and humor, but they are all spoken without rhetorical affectation, in as stripped and bare a form as Racine used, without the music of Racine.

Caligula is about an idea, articulated by the emperor himself: *"Les hommes meurent et ils ne sont pas heureux."* The thought of men dying without being happy is reasoned throughout the entire play until its most extreme consequences are reached. This is the doctrine of existentialism, which in the particular philosophy of Camus treats of existence as something "absurd." Experience is irrational and unjustifiable. The discovery of the absurd in existence is the most decisive moment in a man's life, and when an emperor reasons thus, the results will be tragic and far-reaching.

The first act of *Caligula* is a kind of summation of all four acts. Caligula returns from three days' wandering about the countryside and looks at himself in a large mirror. (The absence of a mirror in *Huis Clos* is as important as the presence of a mirror in *Caligula*.) At the end of the act, when he realizes that his life is being plotted against, he calls in the patricians and reflects himself, in a demented state, in the same mirror. The works of Camus all gravitate around the problem of whether life is worth being lived or not. This is why he chooses Sisyphus as the central myth, and why in his essay he can write: *"Juger que la vie vaut ou ne vaut pas la peine d'être vécue, c'est répondre à la question fondamentale."* [1]

(4)

The first years of the existentialist movement were given over to the metaphysical problems. In the new drama the problems are becoming more recognizably ethical. It is quite clear that the existentialists do not believe in the reliability of reason, nor in the immortality of the spirit, nor in the transcendency of God, nor in any spiritual progress of man. Men exist but there seems to be no apparent reason for their existence.

[1] *Mythe de Sisyphe*, p. 15.

Existence, when described and analyzed, appears essentially "contingent" for Sartre and "absurd" for Camus.

Yet, the secret of human liberty, for the existentialists, seems to lie in the absurd or the contingent. In Simone de Beauvoir's essay *Pyrrhus et Cinéas* every project is analyzed as being a perpetual surpassing of the present. M. Sartre, in a recent lecture, defined the verb "to exist" by the phrase, "to sketch the future" (*"esquisser le futur"*). The eternally superfluous quality of existence has been discovered by the French existentialists in the writings of some American novelists with whom they feel close affiliation: Hemingway, Faulkner, Dos Passos and Steinbeck. The impression of the irremediable, already outlined in the American novels, especially in those of William Faulkner, has deepened in the French existentialist theatre. As in the myth of Sisyphus, so totally applicable to this philosophy, it is possible to continue existing and even working, to continue leading a multiple life, provided one understands and accepts its vanity. Sisyphus can continue rolling up hill his infernal rock as long as existence is impossible to deduce or differentiate from the void.

Note 2

The Example of Max Jacob

The symbolism taught by Mallarmé in the latter part of the nineteenth century was essentially the symbolism of objects. Each of the last and most significant sonnets is constructed around an object whose meaning or "symbolism" is concealed in the description: a bit of foam on the ocean, an empty room, lace curtains, a sunset. There is a human reference in each of the sonnets, but it is always made to the poet, to the man who, according to Mallarmé, fails in the artistic re-creation of his drama. This school of Mallarmé and the symbolism of objects was followed, about the opening of the twentieth century, by the school of clowns, by those artists who discovered in the clown the symbol of man.

The world, seen by the new artists as a disintegrating force, was described by them as a circus nightmare, in which the comic was perpetually being confused with the tragic, in which disaster was projected by fantasy. In Proust's novel, the laughter of Mme. Verdurin is juxtaposed with the suffering of Swann. In Rouault's paintings, the face of his clowns, a supreme example of the new burlesque-tragedy, resembles the face of his prostitutes and of his Christs. In the writings of Max Jacob, satire on the bourgeoisie, buffooneries and a religious conversion cohabit naturally, as if the world of extremes were the new ambiency for the clown-hero.

Max Jacob is the type of modern mystic who reveals himself by means of a burlesqued fantasy in which he can permit himself every form of adventure, even the love of God. He is an example of the man who is embarrassed by having come upon a profound part in his own being, whose face bears the inwardly turned expression of the clown. The center of the world is his heart, but it beats so faintly that he never listens to it. His own heart is hostile and foreign to himself. This clown's heart is the source of the new poignant fantasy created by Jacob, and which can be rediscovered today in the paintings of Marc Chagall, where donkeys, violins, angels and roses form patterns whose beauty is the incongruous, and in the nightmares of Donald Duck, where the universe is pulverized.

The fantasy of Max Jacob, when taken over by the masters, becomes an art of explosion, as in the novels of Léon Bloy and in the paintings of Rouault. The religious theme, absent from the symbolism of Mallarmé, dominates the new circus school. Cocteau's letter to Maritain is its manifesto, and the writings of Max Jacob form one of its most authentic testimonials. The complaints of Laforgue's Pierrot and Jarry's *Ubu Roi* of 1897, helped to consecrate the break with the "poetic" subjects of symbolism and instituted the new tragic fantasy of the circus, where the real spectacle is always performed before God.

After a Breton childhood in Quimper, where he was born of Jewish parents in 1876, Max Jacob came to Montmartre, and there grew into his legend of bohemian, art critic, poet and friend of Picasso. In 1901, Picasso said to him: *"Tu es le seul poète de l'époque."* Max occupied a room at number 7, rue Ravignan, and Picasso lived at number 13. No sunlight ever entered the room at number 7, where a smoking lamp burned night and day. The rue Ravignan became the center of what was referred to as *"la bande Picasso."* Max Jacob and Picasso, André Salmon and Juan Gris, and perhaps especially Guillaume Apollinaire often disturbed the sleep of quieter inhabitants of the rue Ravignan, and ever since have been disturbing the aesthetics and poetic sensibilities of modern artists. Jacob's *Cornet à dés* (1917) helped give rise to cubism and dadaism in its theory that art is essentially distraction (or diversion). In his *Art Poétique* (1922), he announced that Picasso and Reverdy are more Christian than Maurice Denis, and that Racine is as Christian as Bossuet. His life and his writings, his theories and his example all played parts in the emergence of surrealism, which appears today in all the arts as one of the most significant efforts of man's liberation.

On September 22, 1909, at four in the afternoon, in his room at 7, rue Ravignan, Max Jacob had his first vision, which later he explained as being almost the sole reason for his conversion to the Catholic Church. The second apparition, on December 17, 1914, took place in a cinema, where he claimed that Christ, dressed in a white robe, sat down beside him. The following year, on February 18th, Max Jacob received the sacrament of baptism and the baptismal name of Cyprien. He chose as godfather his closest friend, Pablo Picasso. Soon he went to live in a monastery, at Saint Benoît-sur-Loire, where he occupied three cells: one for sleeping, one for his *gouaches* and one for his luggage. During the German occupation he was incarcerated in the concentration camp at Drancy, where he died in May, 1944, after expressing to the Jewish friends who were taking care of him, his wish for a Catholic burial. *"Vous comprenez, j'ai donné ma vie à cette Passion,"* were among his last words.

Max Jacob was one of several converts among writers of his generation: Ghéon, Psichari, Du Bos, Rivière, Marcel, Maritain, Reverdy, Péguy, Claudel. His life was the prodigal son's. His art was the buffoon's, in which disorder was a saving grace. Rimbaud had revealed the new credo in his sentence: *"Je finis par trouver sacré le désordre de mon esprit."* To the generation of Mallarmé, interested in the symbolism of objects, succeeded the generation of Max Jacob, men born between 1870 and 1880, who turned their interest to the symbolism of man and found themselves involved in a circus exhibitionism. Jacob became the most histrionic of his generation. He changed from bohemian to mystic, from Montmartre to Saint Benoît-sur-Loire, and then changed back from saint to sinner, from the cell to the Lapin Agile. The clown's vocation is partly angelic. He causes laughter through understanding the source of joy and through enacting the innocency of man.

INDEX

Anouilh, 18
Apollinaire, 113
Aquinas, 35, 58–9
Auden, 86
Augustine, 76

Balzac, 38
Baudelaire, 34, 37, 44, 62–4, 68, 80–5, 90, 91, 99, 100
Bergson, 10, 57, 58, 75
Bloy, 33–5, 38, 58, 68, 112
Boccaccio, 61
Bos, Du, 114
Bossuet, 46, 113

Camus, 47–9, 107, 109–11
Cézanne, 32, 42
Chagall, 60, 112
Chanel, 18
Chaplin, 99, 100
Chirico, 22, 23
Claudel, 41, 48, 59, 64, 86, 114
Cocteau, 18–23, 29, 45, 66–8, 109, 113
Corneille, 10
Crane, Hart, 100

Dante, 44, 62–4, 82–5, 88, 89, 98, 99
Daumier, 37
Delaunay, 30
Denis, 113
Derain, 31

Descartes, 66, 67, 75
Donne, 88
Dos Passos, 111
Dostoievsky, 34, 65
Dreyfus, 10
Dullin, 18

Eliot, 42–4, 86, 96–9

Faulkner, 111
Favre, G., 57
Favre, J., 56
Flaubert, 40, 41
Freud, 23

Gabin, 47
Gauguin, 104
Gautier, 96
Ghéon, 114
Gide, 19, 41
Gourmont, 35
Goya, 37
Green, J., 65
Greene, G., 47
Gris, 113

Halévy, 10
Heidegger, 48–50, 107
Hemingway, 49, 111
Hirsch, 29
Homer, 74
Honegger, 18
Hugo, 8, 10, 95

Jacob, M., 111–14
Jarry, 113
Jaurès, 10
Joyce, 45, 48, 85
Jung, 23

Kafka, 48, 49, 73, 74, 107
Kant, 75
Kierkegaard, 48–50, 107

Laforgue, 113
Latini, 98
Lautréamont, 39
Lazare, B., 10

Mallarmé, 11, 12, 16, 41, 93–9, 111–14
Malraux, 47
Marcel, 50, 114
Maritain, J., 22, 42, 53–76, 113, 114
Maritain, R., 56
Matisse, 31, 41, 46
Mauriac, 28, 38, 45–8, 64, 65, 68
Modigliani, 32
Moreau, 30–2, 59

Nerval, 90
Nietzsche, 71

Péguy, 1–24, 57, 59, 69, 74–6, 114
Perse, St.-John, 48, 86, 87, 89–91
Picasso, 18, 31, 42, 46, 113, 114

Proust, 41, 45, 48, 112
Psichari 10, 56–8, 114

Racine, 10, 64, 109, 113
Renan, 56
Reverdy, 113, 114
Rilke, 86
Rimbaud, 16, 37, 48, 59, 62, 68, 86, 89–97, 100, 114
Rivière, 114
Rouault, 25–51, 59, 69, 73, 74, 109, 112

Salmon, 113
Sartre, 19, 45, 48, 49, 50, 106, 107, 111
Satie, 68
Severini, 60
Shakespeare, 44, 64
Sophocles, 14, 18, 19, 74
Steinbeck, 111
Stravinsky, 68

Tolstoi, 71
Toulouse-Lautrec, 37

Utrillo, 32

Valéry, 41
Varèse, 91
Verlaine, 95, 96
Vigna, Pier della, 83, 84, 99
Vigny, 40, 41, 95
Virgil, 88, 89
Vlaminck, 31, 32

Wagner, 68